History of the Punjabees

About the Author

Prof. J. N. Nanda is a distinguished writer and a scientist. He was awarded the 2008 distinction of "An Eminent Scientist" by the Science and Culture Forum of the Panjab University, Chandigarh. In the past he was invited to inaugurate a session at the International Conference of Washington D.C. on the Unity of Science. He has been the leader of Government participation in International conferences in Australia and U.K. and had invitation visits to London, Tokyo, Prague and USA. He has founded the Secular Life Society of India. He has discovered the existence of large amounts of iron in the moon which has been projected there from the earth and which started the precipitation of the moon so close to the fully formed earth. His book on "Science and Technology in India's Transformation" is now a classic. It was released by the Rashtrapati in 1986. His book "Glimpses of Indian History and Culture" was published by the Bharatiya Vidya Bhavan; other titles from Concept Publishing Company include 'Cooperative Development of Marine Resources', 'Religion and Philosophy for Modern Youth', 'Bengal, the Unique State', 'North East India' and 'Human Eternity : Stone Age to Mustopia'. His major contributions to human advance are :

A philosophy of New Mahayana or the Co-existence of various religious and political organizations.

A commitment to un-adulterated democracy, human rights and global development.

True appreciation of Indian History and Hinduism eliminating the artificial distinction between all inclusive Hinduism and Buddhism, and religion being personalized individual affair without the need of conversion or an abjuration.

History of the Punjabees

Prof. J.N. Nanda

CONCEPT PUBLISHING COMPANY PVT. LTD.
NEW DELHI-110059

ISBN-13:978-81-8069-651-0 ISBN-10:81-8069-651-0

First Published 2010

Published and Printed by

Concept Since 1974

Concept Publishing Company Pvt. Ltd.
Regd. Office:
A/15-16, Commercial Block, Mohan Garden
New Delhi-110059 (India)
Phones : 25351460, 25351794, *Fax* : 091-11-25357109
Email : publishing@conceptpub.com,
Website: www.conceptpub.com

Editorial Office:
H-13, Bali Nagar, New Delhi-110 015, India.

Cataloging in Publication Data-- *Courtesy:* D.K. Agencies (P) Ltd. <docinfo@dkagencies.com>

Nanda, J. N. (Jatinder Nath), 1920-
History of the Punjabees / J.N. Nanda.
p. cm.
Includes bibliographical references (p.).
Includes index.
ISBN 13: 9788180696510 ISBN 10: 8180696510

1. Panjabis (South Asian people)--History. 2. Punjab (India)--History. 3. Punjab (India)--Kings and rulers. I. Title.

DDC 954.00491421 22

PREFACE

The Punjabees spoke many dialects usually understood all over north-west of India. The main group speaking these dialects was occupying the region of the Sapt Sindhu, i.e. the territory between the legendary Saraswati, and five tributaries of the river Sind flowing from Kashmir into India and Pakistan and flowing in combination as Panchnad into Sind (river). The two other rivers of the Sapt Sindhu being the rivers Kabul and Sind itself. This region is now covered by North West India and North Pakistan. Archaeologists have discovered many stone age inhabited sites in India dating from past 60,000 years or so. Settled life in agricultural villages in India was developed first by the Punjabees. The Punjabees occupied the gateway of India from the west. Whole of western India became a single (Punjabi-Gujarati) village and had a flourishing civilization known now as the Harrapan civilization. Later archaeological sites have been found all over the Punjab and extend towards Gujarat and on both banks of the Indus river. In the Harrapan days, the Punjabees must have learnt to believe in supernatural rulers of plants and animals and deified natural blessings and features of the lands they had occupied. Their adoration was for trees, bulls, rivers and mountains. With the mixing of some immigrants from across the Himalayas, i.e. from Kashmir and the Pamir region, the Punjabees became Aryas. They composed the Vedas and Vyas in his hermitage on the banks of the river Beas composed the epic of gigantic size and coverage, the *Mahabharata* describing the events and the environment that led to the legendary civil war involving the whole of the Aryan world, fought at Kurukshetra.

In order to write a history of modern Punjab, one has to expand the canvas to cover the entire ancient history of western India, i.e. west of Yamuna and the desert country of

Rajasthan, that was peopled by Punjabees speaking languages allied to the Punjabi language. The initial common language and culture beginning from the stone age was the Harappan culture and next common culture of the classics was the Aryan culture. The Punjabees when interacted with the people of the Hindu Kush region to the north of the Iranian plateau assimilated their beliefs and name and came to be known as Hindus. The whole process occurred through social intercourse, trade and love of learning. The basic anchor of the people has been humanism and care for others during peaceful life pursuits. The style was of limited horizon of village land, village forests and village level governance. Tribal and village deity and the village *raja* (king) had complete loyalty of the Punjabees. The system was self-contained and self-propagating. There are no memories of conflicts during the Harappan age excepting the invitation sent to Krishna, the patron of the Pandavas of Indraprastha (Delhi) by the Harappans to live among them at Dwarka to help them against a possible threat from the foreign trade rivals. The record of local conflicts during the Vedic age are overwhelming. Punjabees, evidently had only racial arrogance against the forest produce gathering wild tribes. This stayed with them up to recent times when they regarded the Pachadas of the central Punjab as ignorant butts. (The Sansis, dubbed as a criminal tribe by the British were actually freedom loving wanderers usually against the "foreign" rulers but had given good horsemen to Maharaja Ranjit Singh.) The Aryas lived in villages and similar life was led by the non-Aryan Punjabees. There were innumerable kings in the country and a recognized sport of kings was to expand their kingdom at the cost of the neighbours. There was little attention to a larger national state but everyone thought of a large empire of own king. This bane has come down to our times in the so called groupism and partiality for family relations. The internecine warfare and the fierce onslaught of foreigners seeking a toe-hold in the fertile Indo-Gangetic plain perforce made Punjabees fighter. After Alexander's encounter with the Punjab ruler Porus, the Iranian or Greek forces had a contingent of Punjabee mercenaries. They also assisted all empire builders connected with India including the British. In the world war, Punjabees both Muslim and non-Muslim joined the services in droves. After independence and with linguistic reorganization of Indian states the official Punjabi speaking area has shrunk to Punjab (Pakistan) and Punjab (India). The Haryana state and Himachal Pradesh are now officially Hindi speaking states, but the history of the Punjab will continue to be interwoven with that of the entire region of the Punjabees old.

For the benefit of the reader we have added here one modified sketch of the Mughal empire showing the sway of the Punjabees during the middle ages by an irregular black boundary drawn by the author on the outline map of Mughal empire.

Hindu-Buddhist kingdoms along the western borders of India (chiefly centred on Srinagar, Kangra, Sialkot, Bathinda, Bikaner, Sukkur and Mewar) often occupied territories west of Indus. Persians (and their Afghan vassals) sometimes held territories east of Indus. The Punjabees were incessantly involved in these see-saw campaigns. Persian empire held through Buddhist vassals, areas in the Punjab including Lahore in the 6th century A.D. The last Persian excursion was that of Nadir Shah when he sacked Delhi in 1739. Maharaja Ranjit Singh's Lahore empire extended to Afghanistan as did the Indian empires of Mauryas, Guptas, Mughals and the British.

The Punjabees demonstrated very early their practical skills in agriculture, cotton spinning, pottery and agriculture and gave rise to Harrapan and Vedic civilizations. Their spiritual involvement was demonstrated by their own devotion and attachment to Siva worship. Even now most Punjabi villages have a Siva shrine or holy ascetics and Jogis crediting Siva as creator as well as responsive to the needs

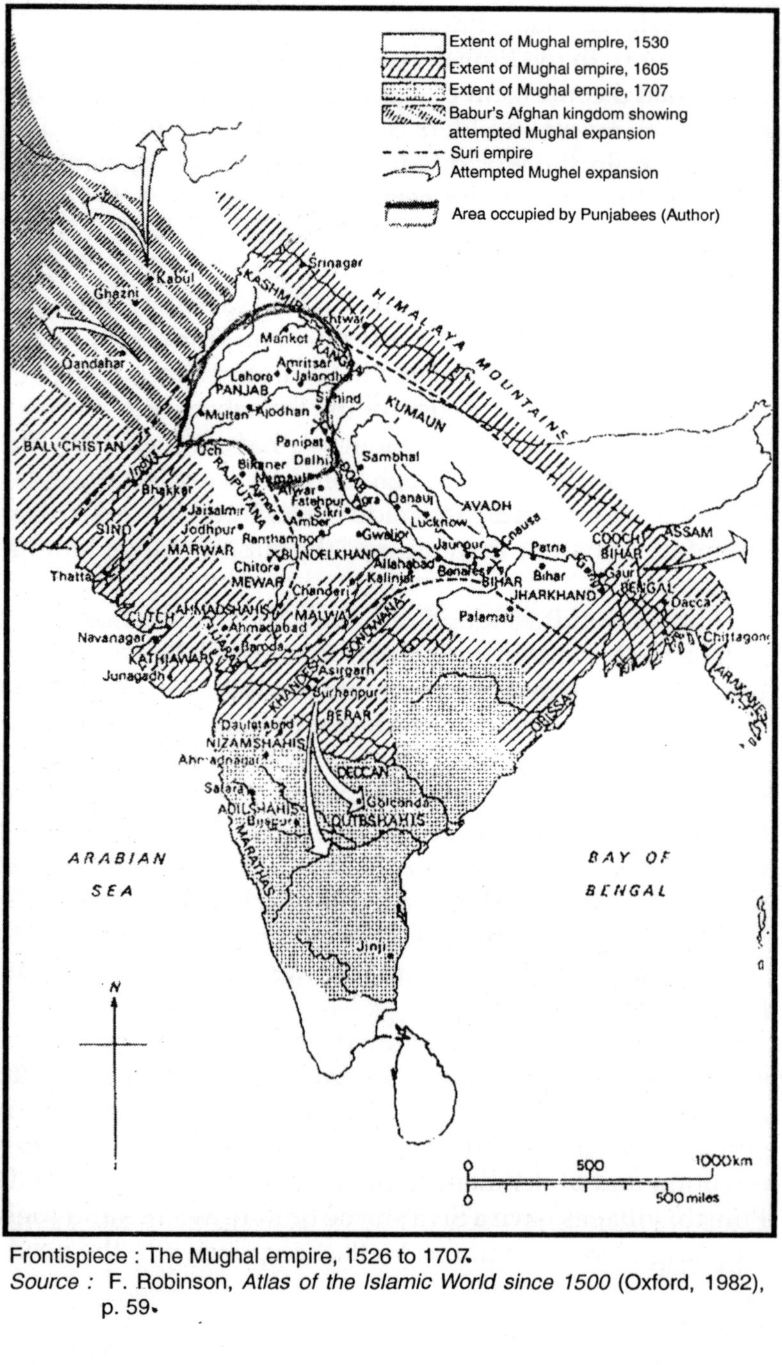

Frontispiece : The Mughal empire, 1526 to 1707.
Source : F. Robinson, *Atlas of the Islamic World since 1500* (Oxford, 1982), p. 59.

of devotees. The Punjabi Hindus developed the idea of man and God being basically the same. They pioneered the ethical foundation of society by promoting Kuru practices, the foundation and predecessor of Buddhist teaching. Punjabees were continuously engaged in war. This led to social cohesion and sometimes to extinction. The Bengalees reached renaissance with the arrival of the British merchants and theologians. In Punjab, British arrived after staging victories over all types of Indians in the rest of India and were experienced enough first to demolish the Sikh empire and then to befriend and also over-awe the Sikhs to help them retake Delhi from the mutineers. The British deliberately set the Indian communities by the ear against each other. When for seven hundred years of Muslim ascendance in most of India there was never a communal riot or exodus of any community from a village or region, but rioting became endemic in British governed India. Revival of Punjab both in India and Pakistan fully describes the indestructible quality of the Punjabees. Ancient warriors are engaged these days in business and accounting. The Aroras, Punjabi speaking group in Haryana constitute a virile community of entrepreneurs. There is the possibility that the Punjab (Pakistan) and the Punjab(India) attend SAARC sessions without the right to vote. Renewed collaboration between India and Pakistan is the aim of all Punjabees. Punjabees are keen to see the victory of Waheguru or truth everywhere. They are keen to see resurgent Indian nation including the federating state of the Punjab flourish with the motto "Truth alone prevails."

The author is indebted to the Punjabi University, Library and publication department as well as the staff of the History Departments of the Panjab University, and the Kurukshetra University for valuable guidance. The notes dispersed in the bibliography at the end of the text are recommended as supplementary to the text. The author wishes to acknowledge the debt he owes to H.E. Dr. A.R. Kidwai, the Governor of

Haryana for assistance in visiting some important sites in Haryana and the Punjab and meeting well known authorities in various universities. He is also indebted to his friend Shri M.S. Batra and Mrs. Batra for help in polishing his Punjabi in Gurumukhi script and some clarifications and contributions by great Sikh scholars after independence to literature, poetry and philosophy in the Punjabi language translated later into other languages.

Once the world resolves to solve all problems by discussion and scientific approach within the scope of democratic freedom and human rights, the Punjabees will be working for the liberation from fanaticism of any kind. Punjabees in India as well as in Pakistan realize that the evolving society has to stay diverse, liberal, democratic and pluralistic. The fundamentalism will be found redundant. This book is written with an eye on future of the Punjab and the Punjabees. We have played down the happenings of partition and hardly included details of Anglo Sikh wars or Anglo Afghan wars that affected the Punjab deeply but subsequent Indian independence and growing realization of inevitable well-being through cooperation of all Indian communities and peace in the subcontinent has convinced us to talk less of past failures when India is building bridges with the whole world. The Punjabees are the best supporters of secularism and cooperative development of the North-West.

Contents

1 INTRODUCTION

1.1 Domain of the Punjabees

The size of the present Punjab (India) or the Punjab (Pakistan) is much less than that of the Punjab of ancient times or even what it was before independence, partition, and the reorganization of the states. The name Punjab stood for the territory through which the five rivers Sutlej, Beas, Ravi, Chenab, and Jhelum, the five eastern tributaries of Indus river, flowed. This would mean Kashmir as well as the part of Indo-Gangetic plain west of the Yamuna (a tributary of the Ganges). When the linguistic reorganization took place in India, Himachal Pradesh and Haryana were separated from the Punjab (India) since the majority of the population in these tracts returned Hindi as their mother tongue. The government of Punjab (India) and the government of India recognizes only Gurumukhi as the script for written Punjabi. Punjabi in Pakistan is written in the Persian script. In India, many would use the Devanagri script for writing Punjabi. Ancient people known as Punjabees lived in the Sapta Sindhu Desh, the part of the Indo-Gangetic plain west of Yamuna watered also by the Indus and the Kabul rivers. Any history of the Punjabees will include the history of the Punjabs (India and Pakistan), Haryana and bordering areas of India and Pakistan to the extant the people there were interacting with the main branch of the Punjabees.

At many places in India, evidence exists of habitations of stone age period from about 100, 000 years in the past. Within Punjab and Gujarat as well as Sind (Pakistan) the relics of a full blown civilization engaged in agriculture, cattle and sheep herding, trading and pottery making are found. Ruins of a town (Mohenjodaro) in Sind and a port town (Harappa) in India have been uncovered. This ancient civilization is known as Harappan cvilization. Their script visible on certain artifacts has not yet been deciphered. The experts speculate their language may be akin to Dravidian languages. Their religion could have been adoration of gods or goddesses looking after the continuation of plants and animals in the forests. They were fond of making clay figures of oxen, trees and folk which appeared to be ascetics. Many adornments for the fair sex are seen among the artifacts. There are also baked clay toys for children. The evidence that is most telling about them is the finding of clay carts and children's toys of that variety still in use in the Punjab villages. Most reliable conclusions of the archaeologists is that the entire Harappan civilization was a Punjabi village of continental size in west India. People were given to pastoral life and pleasure in the abundance provided by nature.

Soon after the introduction of the poetic pursuit of communal worship and singing hymns to the glory of the gods by additional immigrants from Kashmir and the Pamir region beyond the Himalayas, the Punjabees evolved into Aryas. With the evolution of the Punjabees into Aryas, the historical times started for them. There is prolific evidence in the Rig Veda the ancient most culture book of mankind composed in Sanskrit, of the fighting that took place about that time. The Punjabees who had now become Aryas were mainly fighters. Still, some of them were engaged in teaching, learning and practicing the science of longevity along with meditation. The society had recognized the merit of their work and such Brahmans had a special status and privileges. The country was divided into small kingdoms or kingless commonwealths (*Janpads*). Kings or the *Rajas* regarded it as their duty to expand their area of control at the cost of their neighbours, thus aspiring to become *maharajas* or emperors.

In this climate of " might is right", the Punjabees became fighters and were prized for enrolment in the armies of successful empire seekers. As Aryas, they believed in the everlasting souls which transmigrated to different wombs and were re-born.

1.2 Capital Cities of the Punjab

Early history of the Punjab would read like the history of Scottish Clans and other fighting and feuding tribes but for the fact that now and then Punjab had the capital region of empires that extended to the east or to the west. Delhi was part of the Punjab since its founding as Indraprastha in the days of the Mahabharata. Taxila in the west has been an important educational and military centre. Thanesar and Kurukshetra (now in Haryana) have been important pilgrim centres. Harsha, a king of Thanesar, became the head of an empire. He shifted his capital to Kannauj in the present state of U.P. From the third to the sixth century A.D. Dholbaha, a temple city about 30 km. north of Hoshiarpur was a capital city. Delhi has been the capital of India since the Delhi Sultanate and then of the Mughals and the British as well as of free India. It is a Punjab town separated from Punjab as the capital region of India. Indian empires of Mauryas, Kanishka, Harsha, Guptas, and the Moguls ruled also Afghanistan. Ghaznavis of Ghazni through their Sultanate at Delhi ruled over the Punjab. History of Afghanistan and the Punjab are interlinked. The Greek (and Iran) army conquered most of west Punjab and the Shahs of Persia since then laid claim to west Punjab. Their Scythian tribes had often extended their marches to Lahore and Sialkot. The king Saliwahan of Sialkot was Indianized as a hero of the Punjabees when he ousted Persian arms from Multan and his son king Rasalu killed the ruler of Attock and married a princess of Taxila. In the region of salt range, a Greek colony had lasted at Bhera for few centuries.

Kangra, a part of Himachal Pradesh, played a vigorous part in the history of the Punjabees when a Gurkha attack was repulsed at Kangra. Ranjeet Singh's empire covered all the Punjabi areas except some Sikh states between the Sutlej and the Yamuna which separated the Punjabi empire from the domains of the East India Company. Maharaja Ranjeet Singh's Punjab was a secular state under a devout Sikh ruler. Punjab (Pakistan) state has its capital at Lahore which was the capital city also of Maharaja Ranjit Singh's Punjab and had been earlier the seat of the governor appointed by the Mughals or by the Persian Shah. The Indian successor states of the Punjab: Punjab (India) and Haryana have a joint capital at Chandigarh, a union territory.

Delhi since Mahabharata times has been a Punjabi city. It was the capital city of the Sultans and the Mughals. Just before the fall of Delhi to the king of Ghaur, it had a new citadel built by the Tomar Rajputs and the city was part of the Jain confederacy of Delhi-Rohtak-Hissar region and later came under the rule of Chauhans of Ajmer who also were the rulers of Thanesar-Kurukshetra pilgrim centres. Control over the Mughal emperor at Delhi was the prize in the political game played by ambitious players like the Marathas, the Afghans and the British East India Company or their mutinous sepoys. The British could regain control of Delhi from the sepoys in 1857 by their friendship with the local Punjab states not yet incorporated in a united Sikh state. Maharaja Ranjit Singh was also thwarted from incorporating these states already in close embrace of the British. The British Indian province of the Punjab had a territorial expansion after its assistance to the company forces. Agra and Hissar divisions were given over to the Punjab. The Agra division was later taken out to reduce the unwieldy size of the Punjab province. The Punjabees never had a nationalist vision. Many Punjabees south of the Sutlej eyed favourably the lap of the foreigners apparently so comfortable for the ruling feudal faction of the tiny state. After independence in 1947, Punjab

(Pakistan) had been allotted the salt range and Majha area. In addition the fighting bulwark constituted of the Multan-Attock-Taxila lineation and a second Punjabi defence line of Bathinda-Lahore-Sialkot, both happened to be located in Pakistan made a difference in the international trials of strength between the armies of Pakistan and of India. Both found that enmity quickly mounts but is slow to disappear.

1.3 Punjabi Language

A Punjabi characteristic is to switch to their mother tongue even when they are engaged in conversation with a non-Punjabee. Punjabi was the common language of Northern India right up to the Mughal times since people could not very well take to the Persian language which was made the court language by the Sultans and the Mughals, the common folk used a mixed language which came to be known as Urdu. Hindi was the language of the masses. Very similar to Punjabi but used many words derived from Sanskrit. Ranjit Singh's Punjab kingdom favoured Urdu as court language, but freely used spoken Punjabi in the administration. When the British occupied the Punjab, the court language changed from Persian to Urdu but most administrative work was conducted in English. After independence, in principle, the national language for all work is Hindi, but the language of preference of the educated classes, Indian lawyers, Indian physicians, administrators, bankers etc. is English. In fact, persons highly educated in the Hindi medium find much fewer jobs. I have seen a master's degree holder in Hindi praising his luck to land a ball picker's job on the tennis courts used by the Indian educated (and English knowing) elite. Things are slowly changing however as Indians educated in Hindi medium are finding many more vocational avenues but usually some English is expected to be known for jobs at all levels. The Punjabees are in the forefront of Indians knowing and using English for their social and professional work. All higher education in law, medicine, engineering and management is in English medium. Luckily for the current international climate and ideas of one world, India did not follow the Kamal Ataturk's model and banish English from the universities. Now English is the preferred language of classes and even village schools are asking for instruction in the English language. The output of publications, newspapers in English and instruction manuals for new gadgets in English by Indian authors is phenomenal. There is plenty of creative writing and instruction in elementary science and user manuals in Indian languages often using technical terms from the English language. Somehow India has been identified by its moral posturing and spiritual yearnings for health and longevity and within India too, there is considerable demand for books on Indian spiritualism, religious epics, yoga manuals etc. There are books describing assured rewards of superstitious beliefs in astrology, worship of all kinds including prescribed pilgrimages by all religions and attendance at temple festivals and bathing fairs. The Indian language press and publications are full of excellent literature, particularly short stories, poetry and humour at the cost of our politicians and dogmatic obscurantists.

In the Punjab (Pakistan) elementary education is in Urdu. In the past adult education was attempted in Punjabi (Urdu script). The Punjabees everywhere have great affection for the Punjabi language which is evident when they converse or when they recite or listen to Punjabi couplets and exchange Punjabi wit and humour. Punjabi romances and poems like Heer Ranjha or Mirza Sahiban and others are popular. Popular renderings of Puran Bhagat, Raja Rasalu, or Gugga Pir are perpetual favourites. Punjabi crystallized as a language by the popular poetry of Baba Farid and Baba Nanak. Punjabi short stories and one act plays are popular. Sajjad Zahir's renderings draw crowds in both Punjabs. The Punjabi academy of Pakistan has published *dohas and kafias.* Punjab (Pakistan) is likely to establish a Guru Nanak

University at Nankana Sahib, particularly devoted to Punjabi poetry and literature.

1.4 Sources of History of the Punjabees

For ancient history one has to trust speculation on observations and finds through archaeology and archaeological research in other countries or refer to ancient books created in ancient Punjab and Kashmir like the Vedas and principal Shastras of the Aryans. For history of the millennium before and after the birth of Christ one can refer to diaries of Greek ambassadors, Chinese travellers, *Puranas*, old manuscripts saved by temples, royal grants to temples and *maths*, coins, and writings of Greek, Kashmiri and Arab historians. For recent history there are history books, diaries, museums, libraries, archives, monuments, travelogues etc.

The Indian authors usually in old times did not write histories faithfully. They would always switch to the didactic or the panegyric mode. Writing about India the authors from imperialist countries of Europe would write with a bias, all the time highlighting the outlandish customs and characteristics which could have been more sympathetically treated. The history of the Punjab has to be inferred from their books about India and the Hindu kingdoms written by Arabs and the Mughals. Many Punjabees have penned poems and epics on love and life. The folk lore and bardic creations could illuminate some forgotten elements of Punjab History. The *Rig Veda* and the *Mahabharata* composed by the inspired Punjabees are excellent sources. Waris Shah's Heer gives good account of the Punjab situation of his time, and a common respect for Guru Gorakh Nath's disciples. National archives and the archives of the two Punjab states are rich resources. Kalhan's *Rajtarangini* and Baber's *Babar Nama* are good sources. Coins picked up from various places are confirmatory sources.

No historical manuscripts of Punjabi authors have

survived. The learned also looked then towards the imperial masters with their seats outside Punjab. The local chieftains were patronizing only bards and preserved folklore. Punjab events get mentioned in some religious books or Sufi poetic works. Ved Vyas was a Punjab genius and the *Mahabharata* gives considerable information about Punjab and its ruling kings and tribes prominent on the Punjab scene. The Sikh Gurus and many Sufi Pirs taught in Punjabi and refer to the state of the people of the Punjab. Chinese texts and travelogues and of Arab explorers also throw light on the life in the Punjab of their times. An interesting report is from an Arab traveller that the Hindus in Punjab had strange festivals when they celebrate marriage of a stone with a plant.

1.5 Period Classification of the History of the Punjabees

History of India and Indian states is often divided into Hindu, Muslim, colonial and Self-rule periods. The Hindu period is often distinguished from the Buddhist or the Jain Periods. This is only due to the projection, to the past-times of ancient Asian civilizations, of modern European experience of religious cleavage in European countries. Religious cleavage of pastoral cooperative life of Indian villages occurred only after sustained imperial atrocities and misdirection. Hindus never imagined that religion and philosophy could generate exclusivism of any kind. The Jain philosophy whose seeds were strewn in the Vedas was always tentative and advanced with advances in human experience. Similarly Buddhism was based on the genius of a single creative thinker who questioned deeply and discovered answers. Asoka was to Buddhism as St. Peter was to Christianity. He spread far and wide the common humanism of the Hindus, a product of the Punjabees which made coexistence of all forms of worship possible. Hindu, Buddhist or Jain period clearly comes under the broad category of Hindu period where the majority of the population may for that limited time be preferring various kinds of philosophy for intellctual satisfaction. Hindus do not believe in conversion of others to Hinduism. All are born Hindus. Only some do not know it. Punjabees had a long Hindu period and then the Muslim period because of Muslim and Mughal conquest over rulers of Delhi which was the gateway to the rest of India. During the Muslim period, the interaction with west Asia enriched Indian arts, crafts, music etc. in exchange for Indian philosophy, Indian science and technologies. There was a patchwork of Hindu kingdoms coexisting as free states or under treaty obligations to the central all India Muslim power. Indian medieval anarchy led to neglect of science and technology in the pursuit of superstitious attempt to quickly grasp paradise, while Europe despite its religious divide had a renaissance and industrial revolution which inspired them to find markets for their products abroad. European self-assurance allowed them to expand their imperial hold over the world. The Punjab also after a brief interlude of independence and ascendance of secular Sikh rule went under colonial yoke before achieving independence as part of a democratic and resurgent India. In a truly secular state all religions can co-exist with dignity, but there is full scope for reform and democratic empowerment of the people which is unlike the imperial secular rule guaranteeing a lid on religious reform unless it were to suit the imperial rule. The Punjabees too would march ahead along with others to peaceful world and contribute to the establishment of a community advancing to a world utopia (Mustopia) of author's conception.

The Punjab's history thus was begun by Hindus of yore and then by Muslims who for a long time held aloof from the prevailing tolerance. But the Sufis among them like Hazrat Nizam-ud-Din Aulia of Delhi and his famous disciple Amir Khusro had religious beliefs almost akin to those of the Hindus. The British colonial rule was secular in a limited sense that they regarded all Indian religions as equally inferior to Christianity and had no interest in religious reformation of

Indian beliefs. They would side with obscurantism if it suited imperial interests or with change in barbarous practices like *Sati*. Caste fragmentation in India suited the Muslim and the British Empires in India. Free India still needs energetic steps to propagate secularism and national integration. Most recent mountain has been found in a mole-hill by the Akal Takhat when they demanded an apology from a guru of a sectarian society of Bhatinda. The matter is still in the courts and requires to be settled amicably in the interest of many Punjabees who desire to have a living guide in their day-to-day life.

In order to avoid disappointment later, the state must crush all weeds of parochial superiority as displayed by archaic *hukumnamas* or *Sharia orders* against the dignity of the individual. The reform in religion should be free from the holy writ of the religion claiming it to be in no need of improvement. Science and technology is a superior informer and a challenge towards betterment. India can learn from Tunisia how to curb blind *ulema* power in any religion practiced in India. In Tunisia, a Muslim nation, polygamy is illegal while a whiff of freedom for women raises a howl here. The immediate example is the treatment of a secular hero from Bangladesh or the tennis woman star of India.

1.6 Religions in the Punjab

Punjabees profess many religions. There are Hindus including Buddhists and Jains, Sikhs, Muslims, Christians etc. Though separate categorization in the census does not exist, but Punjabees do have Ahmediyas or Qadiani Muslims (regarded as non-Muslims by Pakistani *ulema)*, Sufis, Sahajdhari Sikhs (not recognized as Sikhs by the Sikh *ulema)*, Nanakpanthis. Recently, under the incentive of status improvement, some scheduled caste Hindus have converted to Buddhism. This is apparently under a delusion since Buddhists are not outside Hinduism. Hindus regard the

Buddha as an incarnation of Vishnu like Rama or Krishna and gladly pray in a Buddhist temple. Buddhist principles as they appear on Asoka's edicts are fully accepted as part and parcel of Hinduism. Still they escaped the indignity within Hinduism of being outcastes. Hindus shed the excessive emphasis on non-violence since the Hindus and particularly the Punjabees had to cope with infilterating and on opportunity attacking Persians, Arabs, or Scythians in the wake of Alexander's invasion. They had also to exert for their expulsion where their rule was oppressive.

The neo-Buddhists would like to get rid of caste prejudices of Hindus. The Indian society as a whole is on the same side and is against obnoxious tendencies of casteism. Untouchability has been outlawed. Scheduled caste status is now sought after by some groups in India. The Jains are close to humanism of the ancient Hinduism. The Jain philosophy is founded with a base in the Vedas. Jains are quite modernistic in their discussion of theism. The spiritual advance of a Jain happens only through a pious life and the grace of the everlasting Jain Tirthankers or the evolved souls. Hindus include theists of all kinds as well as atheists. They find it natural to pray to natural bounty, tribal gods and goddesses and they find it most convenient for the straight and narrow path if they have a living guide and also the prop of an idol of their favourite god or goddess to pray to.

Hindus had the system of having a personal guru from ancient practice and do still accept someone who commands respect in society as a personal guru. They do not consider the practice as a revolt against the tenets of their holy books. A living guru can better remove their spiritual doubts and explain the scriptures since the ordinary temple priests have a vested interest in keeping the people ignorant and dependent. The institution of having a personal guru (one could call him by some other epithet) is quite common among Sikhs looking at the popularity and following of the Radha Soamis, Nirankaris and now Sachcha Sauda among the Sikhs.

Sikhism in essence is not much different from Hinduism or Buddhism or other Indian gurudoms like the followers of the saint of Shirdi, who was born a Hindu but was brought up in early life as a Muslim. According to the gurus, Kabir or Baba Farid, piety does not reside in external symbols. The five "K" Sikh symbols are prescribed for the Khalsa, i.e. the Sikh army historically the entire Sikh community (goaded by imperial injustice of the Mughal despotic rule) dedicated to the protection of the weak and a challenge to any aggressor acting against natural justice and against curbs on the exercise of human rights. The Indian army, so long as India pursues the policy of democratic freedom and assurance of equal rights of all, is precisely the Khalsa army of Guru's conception and this way the prediction of the Guru that ultimately the Khalsa will rule the entire country is being fulfilled. The power however lies with democratic leadership of the people and not the priests or attendants at the temples or Gurdwaras or elected managers (*prabandhaks*) on franchise limited to Sikhs who display the symbols of the faith. The national army of India has to have wide base that is whole of India and competitive strength on land, air and the seas. The new Khalsa has to have widest possible science and technology base in the country. The entire population of whole of India has to be engaged in building up an India to approach the state when it was rich and a friend for the entire world. The Indian as well as the Punjab's priorities are security, technology, and proper husbanding of food, water, and fuel resources to become world class trading country as well as holding its own in the give and take of scientific and technological advances. In the quest for social betterment, some scheduled caste Hindus are getting converted to other religions. Dr. Ambedkar favoured conversion to Buddhism noting the obstruction to temple entry for the scheduled caste people and the feeling of inferiority thrust on them by the institutions monopolized by the higher castes. The conversion would get them away from the bully upper castes of Hindus.

The conversion no longer seems necessary. The democratic adult suffrage in the country assures them full share of Indian produce. In addition, already, scheduled caste label has become a badge of preference in India. The new political power of the scheduled castes, in alliance with upper class Brahmans in Uttar Pradesh, is a pointer towards the all India environment of the coming decades. Fortunately the disabilities of scheduled classes were being attended to by the religious and political leaders of the Punjab since the reforming zeal of Guru Nanak and Swami Dayananda whose teachings found good soil in the Punjab. The Harijan uplift movement of Mahatma Gandhi was very successful in the Punjab.

The Jain philosophy is hinted at, in the Vedas. Jains are quite modern in their estimation of theism. They pray to Tirthankers, the developed souls for guidance in their meditation. They extol asceticism and celebrate most events by observing a fast. They go to considerable pain to avoid killing of even insects. They wear masks over their mouth to filter the air they breathe. The Digamber Jains do not wear clothes as a part of perpetual penance. K.M. Munshi has written a lot about the medieval period achievements of Jains in his series of historical novels "Gujarat Ke Nath". Jains have prospered all over India. The Jains ruled the south-eastern part of the Punjab including Delhi and lost to the Rajputs and later to the Pathans. Slowly they have shifted to the mercantile profession. Aroras are ancient fighters of the Punjab like the Agarwals and both of these castes of Hindus are very close to Jains. Many businesses in India are handled by Jain, Arora, and Agarwal families. The rest of the Hindus of the Punjab include Jats concentrated in Haryana are engaged mostly in agriculture and village industries including animal husbandry. Khatris, the fighters of old, have taken to the un-ostentatious shop-keeping. Up to the middle of 18th century every village in west India (present Pakistan) and in Afghanistan as well as the villages of the Oxus region beyond the Hindu Kush contained a Khatri owned shop-*cum*- money lending business. Hindus of the Punjab are mostly Sahajdhari Sikhs. The communal award gave concessions to Sikhs beyond their proportion in the head count and the Sahajdhari Sikhs could not have any such advantage. Now that all citizen of the Punjab have equal rights, the Hindus look beyond the Punjab since their high education and professional commitment makes them welcome immigrants everywhere. Most Punjabi Hindus are given over to modern Bhakti cults of gurus, of Rama, Krishna, or of the various Devis, and of Hanuman. They believe in the existence of a cosmos of gods, the chief gods being Brahma, Shiva and Vishnu. The ever expanding Bhakti cult is the most common religion. They commonly worship Siva and Shakti, Rama or Krishna. They have inherited the essence of ethics as well as the catholicity of the Mahayana and believe in the coexistence of all living beings. Punjabees love to sing and listen to Waris Shah's Heer and hear the stories of Gugga Pir and Raja Rasalu heroes of whole Punjab. Only after independence is India in a position to provide state support to common Indian philosophy and culture of humanism, secularism and democratic freedom of the individual.

1.7 Pockets of Fundamentalism

Indian culture is of the middle path. Fundamentalism is opposite of liberalism. Indian culture primarily of coexistence and freedom of belief and expression abhors fundamentalism. Still some pockets of fundamentalism persist. One is in Kashmir. So long as Kashmiri Pandits forced to be refugees outside their native land are not induced to return, the fundamentalism of the state will persist giving sustenance also to the Hindu revivalist sentiment in Jammu. A different fundamentalist sentiment for a Naga empire in the north east India has arisen simply because democratic majority in the north east is over dependent on the Central Government at Delhi to satisfy various tribal minorities encouraged by the centre to raise their demands when the initial ones had been accepted in full by agreeing to give state status to all viable distinctive cultural regions of the area. A further Balkanization will be counter productive to the region's advancement. Being a large country, India with the consent of its constituent states, should be ready to try new experiments. A regional super state can be granted direct trade relations with certain foreign countries which can help the components feel the new environment of globalization and self-fulfilment in planned development according to their genius. With the advances continuing in the infrastructure and financial solidity of India, the fundamentalism of major communities will soon vanish like a painful dream let loose by the partition riots.

1.8 Dealing with Fundamentalism

The integrating efforts are well supported by the projects and policies of the central and state governments. Crimes and scams that endanger integration and development should be nipped in the bud. The handling and the start of the Dera affair was rather *ad hoc*. The law of the land and rulings of the court are the proper referees. The country can have full capability to discourage frivolous *bandhs*, massive political gatherings just to impress the law enforcing agencies (usually with the same idle crowd). In a democracy, perhaps certain TV channels could be assigned to major protesters in the country so that the government can argue on the screen with them through debating non-officials. The style of political processions that had to be used during the freedom struggle should now give place to different head counting protests which TV channels can manage. Any interference with internal means of communication like blocking rail or road traffic and burning of buses and damaging public property has to be severely *dealt* with and the offenders including the so called leaders have to be pursued for punishment till it is administered to them by summary prosecution and judgement. Raj Thackerey who instigated the Maharashtrian mobs against north Indian residents of Mumbai, a clear insult to nationalism of Indians, is still unrepentant. Son of the soil agitationists and other fundamentalists will soon come down from their lofty stand and come to terms with the thinking in India of the common man. The budding coalition of the dalit party and high caste Brahmans in Uttar Pradesh is a pointer to the new awakening in India.

The stage has arrived when the next constitutional amendment passed properly by both the houses of the parliament should proclaim a stop to all kinds of reservation whether in government or private service or in educational institutions. The government should act in the interest of all including the aspirants from backward classes and communities by liberally providing them educational and training stipends so that at the competition and the selection stage, only observed merit of a candidate for the job requirement should count. Any special interest which has to be progressed in the wisdom of the elected government should be picked up and employed ex cadre for a set limited period. Let India also take to secularism as fundamentalists pursue their chosen faith. The central authority must have no second thought when punishing the elements opposed to the development of India along the constitutional guidelines. Personal law has to be codified and applied to all Indian citizens taking a cue from Tunisia (a modern Islamic state) who have outlawed polygamy for its citizens most of whom are Muslims. Parochial organizations in the industrial and educational fields have to be discouraged since it is difficult to outlaw them later. We have bitter experience of Islamic students federation and Sikh students federation and similar religion and caste based organizations, e.g., the Gujjar Maha Panchayat. India has to learn to wade across such efforts to split social categories along non-secular lines. The parliament which is democratically elected and popular parties and leaders should have easy channels of mass communication so that they are more effective in the national interest. It is about time to re-open the *Shah Bano case* in which the obscurantists were allowed to reverse the court verdict. The administration of a large country requires continuous regard for the nation's viability and down sizing of any communal or caste considerations. Sooner we get out of the mess created by religious and caste basis, better would it be for progress of all Indians. For a continuous secular improvement in all directions important steps like freedom of being informed has been made a legal right. For the spread and ready availability of information, intelligent advances in television programmes, internet accessibility and computer education have to be made and taken out of controversies of language and script keeping always a reserve language and script used all over the world. Computer utilization should progressively be taught in village schools overcoming the confusion which may develop if we continue to harp on the use of Indian alphabets and Indian languages for computer instructions.

Indian courts have given the lead many times to requirements of nation building. Let secularists also become fundamentalist, not permitting merit to be swamped by mediocrity. Science, technology, mathematics, bio-technology etc., the sinews of progress all require the best experienced and trained minds. Let us not thwart merit for faults of the political immaturity. The need is not only that truth prevails, but also of the law to prevail. The central authority must not be lenient to any Taliban like activity in any Indian group. All clergies should be judged by their actions for integration and for action for reforming their religion according to the proven findings of scientific approach.

1.9 History as Guide

The history of the Punjabees will bring forth the humanism and tolerance, the steadfastness and courage, the sacrifices in the common interest that human beings are capable of. The Punjabees opened the subcontinent of India to civilized living. Agriculture was the primary culture they specialize in. The other is the ideal of a saint soldier lived by the great Guru Govind Singh.

Half of India is strewn with archaeological sites pertaining to ancient Harappan civilization which must have started in Punjab and spread in ancient lands of Balochistan, Gujarat, and the land of the Pushtuns. Punjabees also created the Aryan civilization which spread into India and attracted modern Europeans. Earlier the Hindu-Buddhist culture spread over whole of ancient Asia. India can progress only through democracy and coexistence. The Indian state has to suppress all offences against national integration and human rights using the resources of electronic media and intellectual debate. The Punjabees will be in the fore-front of advancement of the world to governance by a democratic world federation (reformed UN) and reaching a worldwide Mustopia for the whole of mankind.

2 PUNJAB, THE KEY STATE

2.1 Introduction

The Punjab state of India is only a part of the area occupied by the Punjabees. A large part is now the Punjab state of Pakistan (Punjab P). The partition of India happened on the ground only after the Punjab got the Unionist ministry there expelled and governor's rule installed. The partition riots were most intense in Pakistan and particularly in the Punjab (P) and drew retaliation most severely in the Punjab (I). The civil war prone Punjabees were at it with all possible zeal. Fanaticism begets fanaticism. The fanaticism of the masses led by the illiterate mullahs in rural Pakistan was fanned to white heat by the British overlords through their mistaken reading of the future of religious minorities in India. The founder President of Pakistan, Mr. M.A. Jinnah himself came to regard partition of India as a mistake if the Muslim nation of Pakistan was to give up secularism and deny democratic rights to all its citizens. It was the political hatred between the two nations that drove them to acquire nuclear weapons. India had to arm itself reluctantly because of the saber rattling by both Pakistan and China. Both these countries laid claim to Indian territory. The events turned up strangely. The Chinese attacked India but found the exercise a futile one when a reasonable neighbourly relationship could be developed. The territorial claims remaining hanging in the air, the two sides are still arguing their case in conferences along with discussions regarding the demarcation of international boundary which should not be difficult if only the mutual territorial claims are whittled down.

The U.S.A. supported the Pakistan based Afghan defence against Soviet interference in Afghan affairs. Earlier, the American military push in Vietnam was convincingly defeated by the spirited defence of the communists of Vietnam. The outcome was increased expectations from the United Nations, which rose to the occasion when Iraq attacked Kuwait. Later when USA attacked Iraq on trumped up charges regarding illegal preparation of weapons of mass destruction, the weakness of the UN was very much visible.

Islamic anger at the intransigence of Israel and slow destruction of Arab Palestine and the continued harangue from Pakistan about the imperialist hold of India over a Muslim majority Kashmir state, culminated in the declaration of Islamic *Jehad* by the terrorists entrenched in various outfits in Pakistan which burst in the form of renewed *Taliban* attacks on free Afghanistan and terrorist attacks using suicidal jet planes hitting the US World Trade Center in New York. The world became aware of the danger to civilization from fanatic Muslim terrorists and relative ineffectiveness of the Security Council of the UN. The policy alternatives before various countries were now laid out afresh and the stance of various countries is now becoming clear. USA was the first to wake up. The USA will be friend with Pakistan but not at the cost of India. Pakistan has announced their joining in the hunt of terrorists with the proviso of not stopping aid and moral support to *jehadists* fighting for the liberation of Kashmir from its constituent position in India. USA is also going to strengthen its friendship with India and has plans to support it in attempts to meet power needs through atomic reactors. India and Pakistan have also agreed to explore further avenues of neighbourly cooperation except that Pakistan will not hand over any Islamists alleged to have been involved in terrorist attacks in India or in Kashmir.

2.2 Two Punjabs Together

Now is the time to clear one's goals. What are the best efforts that the two Punjabs can make for achieving the national goals and policies. Pakistan would formulate its intentions afresh when the current constitutional issues are resolved. Will the democracy be in ascendance. New elections could bring back a new prime minister out of Benazir Bhutto, Nawaz Sharif or the controversial suspended Chief Justice. Or the new president other than Musharraf may wish to steer away from the failed policies of the past and attempt to be sincere in the re-approachment with India. The Punjab (P) has almost the opportunity of the century to help the country make the choice that will bring credit and affluence through self-help to both the countries. India still regards Pakistan as a brother who had been estranged. There are always easy and friendly relations of Punjabees irrespective of the side of the international border, their native residence is or used to be. The two Punjabs have to develop cordial relations through trade and travel. Further efforts through SAARC should succeed if representatives function in respective embassies particularly in UAE, Sri Lanka and Bangladesh in order to bolster Punjab-Punjab trade and culture. Both Punjabs would favour strengthening the UN and sorting out the problem of West Asian stability. Both would want a guaranteed premier position of Iran in the middle east. Before Alexander's invasion of the Punjab, a strong state in the Punjab(P) area existed of King Porus of Jhelum. Earlier, a kingdom ruled by Pakkusate of northern Punjab sent ambassadors to Media and Chaldea. An Iranean expeditionary force overcame the resistance of the Punjabees in 528-515 B.C. when they occupied Multan as well as Lahore. Trading blows and giving refuge to each other's rebels and refugees was a common feature of Iran-Punjab history besides commercial, cultural and technological exchanges. (Lahore and Kasur were founded by Luv and Kush, the sons of Rama, the legendary hero of the Ramayana.)

The two Punjabs can cooperate in setting up joint institutions regarding flood control, and nuclear energy plants. The proposed Guru Nanak University in Pakistan could have a department of practical experiments with the Guru's Teaching and ethical aphorisms. Both could hold seminars on the Guru's assertion *"na koi Hindu na koi Mussalman"* which will do good to all mankind. Pakistan's general election after the assassination of Benazeer Bhutto has brought back democracy and rule of law.

2.3 Punjab (I) : A Symbol of India

The Punjab state of India truly represents the country. The Punjabees are renowned fighters; they have a sense of humour and make excellent friends or feuding foes. Most of them are Sikhs and are ever ready to come to the aid of the needy. Sikhism shorn of any ritualism that has crept in, reflects the deepest insights of Hinduism. The Gurus rejected asceticism which is extolled in all Indian philosophies. The Guru taught that life of virtue and dedication must be lived while living in one's family. The Punjab (I) with 1.5 per cent area produces 20 times required wheat and is known as the granary of India. The Punjab produces 2 per cent of the world's cotton production. It has 200,000 small scale industrial units. Punjab (I) has 1000 microhydal projects. This is the recommended step for cutting down the construction of large dams for irrigation purposes. Punjab is busy with the construction of a quark city and an IT park at Mohali near Chandigarh for increasd employment opportunities for the increasing crop of electronics and IT engineers. They are developing a knitwear cluster and a bicycle cluster for the manufacture of machines and machine parts at Ludhiana. (Ludhiana has developed as the Manchester of India.) The Ranjit Sagar dam, a part of a multi-purpose river valley project will soon be attracting tourists upstream of the Madhopur canal, among other benefits. The re-modelling of the Upper Bari Doab Canal is planned.

The Punjab (I) like all other states of India is also a land of picturesque fairs, e.g. Basant fair in spring season at Patiala,

Hola Mohalla at Talwandi Sabu or the Roza Sharif at Sirhind and Baisakhi fair at Achchal tank of Batala, Shaikh Farid Fair at Faridkot and the Harballabh Sageet Sammelan at Jalandhar draw large crowds. In addition there are government sponsored heritage festivals which are very popular with the tourists and the Punjabees living overseas. These fairs are routinely held at Amritsar, Patiala and Kapurthala. The Punjab (I) has seen the rise and fall of the Mauryan empire, of Greek, Kushan and Gupta empires.

They believe in the Guru's blessing that Khalsa (the army of the virtuous and the defenders of justice) will be victorious ultimately. They pin their faith on a truly successful Security Council of the U.N. The Punjab population has crossed twenty-five million and this figure should be doubled for Punjabees if we add the present population of Haryana and Himachal Pradesh to it. One should visit Magh Mela at Muktesar or the prayer crowds at Beas Satsang to get a feel of Punjab's disciplined crowds.

The Punjabees in their Indian villages subdued two attacks of modernized Pakistani army even when they must have attacked in cohorts with their imperialist mentors. Pakistan distributed chickens of victory even before they were hatched when they gave away a slice of Kashmir to China and this is in part bedeviling the India-China border settlement. USA and its allies desperately needed Pakistan's space for their plans against the pressure southwards in Asia of the Soviet Union. After the collapse of the Soviet Union and democracy and nationalism sweeping across the continents, the new world problem is of aggressive *Jehadist* terrorism launched by much aggrieved Muslim leaders. The *Jehad* rhetoric is chiefly at present against the USA for their support of Israeli intrusion into Palestine, against Russia for not allowing Chechenyan Muslim majority to secede and against India for not permitting Kashmir to secede when the majority of Kashmiris throughout their History have preferred to cast their lot with India and now too they as

Indian citizens enjoy full freedom plus regard from other Indians for their Rishi (Sufi Muslim) religious leadership and nationalism. With changes in the international climate and the perennial interest in just peace of India, USA is finding itself close to India who has welcomed working with USA and Pakistan against international terrorism. The success of new policy will depend on the coming new Pakistan government's handling of their own entrenched fanatic groups engaged in terrorist adventures within Pakistan and outside. They are engaged in reviving Taliban against Afghan's legitimate government and infiltrating in support of disgruntled voices in Indian Kashmir. The rebels there are the ones deliberately introduced into Kashmir by the compliance of official machinery of Pakistan. Most of them however now surrender there with their weapons. In the meanwhile by their joint efforts, India-Pakistan political friendship is growing particularly in new SAARC initiatives. The climate is favourable for further peace and development efforts from the two Punjabs. Desired progress in South Asia will soon come about when there is clearer perception of Iran's aims and self-estimation in the US and the UN. Iran is heir to the greatness of Alexander and Darius. Iran had close relations with India. Many Iranian hard-pressed minority communities have found refuge for centuries in India and have prospered as Indian citizens. Many a refugee king or prince of India found aid and succor in Iran. Iran and India had the original Aryan flowering of culture and both have pious Muslim populations that regards many sites in the middle east as well as in India as their holy places. In short India and Iran are friends and have interest with Pakistan to have Iran oil and gas flow to Pakistan and India. India is willing to trust Iranian zeal for atomic energy being only for peaceful purposes. The world is now too strong for a lone wolf in sheeps' pen when guarded by the powers like those of Russia and the USA. India is happy to be optimistic about expansion of nuclear energy production in India to a desired minimum extent but nuclear energy is beset with problems of public acceptance and increasing difficulty with time of waste disposal in spite of estimated future technological progress. Half of Punjab has been in Iran's possession in the past just as Indian empires have been treading on Iran's toes. During the Mughal period of Indian history, many arts and technologies and medical and other knowledge were freely exchanged between India and Iran. Indian scholars of Persian have been widely respected. Persian was a court language in the Punjab up to recent times.

2.4 Punjab's Excellence

Punjabees are considered the hope of Indian sports. Punjab and Haryana contribute disproportionate number of volunteers for recruitment into the army. They brave the inclement weather to man northern defences and often have peace keeping duty not only in the occasional disturbed border districts of the east but also abroad. Though the Punjab is very much an inland state, yet the number of Punjabees that sail in Indian naval vessels is astounding. Punjabees have risen to highest civil and military ranks. Dr. Salaam Punjabee is the recipient of *Nobel Prize for Physics* in Pakistan. Punjabees in India as well as Pakistan have made a crowning niche in literature and dramatics, films and music. The Punjabees have made homes in many lands and have brought such foreign countries closer when the people overseas observe the law abiding ways of the Punjabees and their easy participation in the community life. Ancient Punjabees, (but now recognized as Hindi speaking as a result of lingering inter-communal politics) have prospered in free India. Gurgaon in Haryana next door to Delhi is regarded as the corporate capital of India. Haryana has launched many technology parks and has about a hundred thousand industrial units. They have developed a petro-chemical complex at Panipat. The culture and pilgrim centre of

Kurukshetra has now got excellent facilities for tourists and pilgrims. The museums and visual displays of episodes of Mahabharata have been beautifully made educative and instructive. Haryana boasts of being the first state in India to provide 100 per cent electrification of villages. Haryana has pioneered in lift irrigation. They have many young universities and technical institutions. In time the spread of higher education will give dividends.

Delhi, the capital city of the Aryas and the capital city of the Pandavas as well as the Sultans and the Mughals or the British in India, is still the capital now of free India. Delhi is known as the garden city of India. It has innumerable monuments. Delhi is well known as the home of Khwaja Nizamuddin, of Amir Khusro and the most loved poet Ghalib. The Qutub Minar, Bahai temple, Red Fort, Jama Masjid, the new incarnation of the Akshardham temple are among many architectural attractions. The chief industry of Delhi besides excellence in many handicrafts, is running the Government of India. The Chief Justice of India and the chiefs of the three armed services also have their headquarters at Delhi. The parliament and the information and media services crowd Delhi with participants, visitors, and viewers. Delhi is the principal Punjabee city of India. The pre-independence cities of Lahore and Bombay merge in it. Soon the shortcoming of a film city may be eliminated when one is established in its neighbourhood at NOIDA of Uttar Pradesh.

Pahari dialect speaking Himachal Pradesh (Pahari would be as much a dialect of Punjabi) also is progressing as a new state with the merger of many small states of the Himalayan approaches. There is flourishing horticulture and export of ornamental plants and medicinal herbs. The population is enthusiastic in the worship of gods of the Hindu pantheon. Each village has its favourite god. The Dussehra festival at Kullu is famous when the gods from many villages gather to honour Shiva, the chief of the gods. Dharamsala is a well known health resort close to Kangra which has ruins of an old fort and a living tradition of worship of the goddess of fire. It has the only fire temple of India (not connected with Zoroastrianism). There is everlasting flame in the temple shrine from a vent in the earth spewing forth combustible gases. Hoshiarpur district of old Punjab was merged with Himachal for providing them more agricultural land and for setting up various educational and other institutions as part of development of the state. Kangra and Hoshiarpur have been ancient bastions of the Punjabees. Traces of Palaeolithic and pre-historic habitations exist there. Hoshiarpur constituted the conduit of Aryan culture between Himalayan Vedic nests and the Punjab.

Punjabees have a great future in democratic and secular India, once the sectarian short-sightedness is overcome in the two Punjabs, the tone setters now for the rest of the Pakistan and India. The marching together of India and Pakistan with other members of the UN will be good for the future *Mustopia*, the ultimate objective of the human civilization, as envisaged by the author.

3 PRE-HISTORIC PUNJAB

3.1 Introduction

Dr. Arun Keshwani of Kurukshetra University while addressing the Punjab History Congress has summarized the Punjab's significance in pre-History. He states that there is no doubt, from the study and analysis of the findings in the Punjab's pre-historical sites that the Punjabees gave rise to two civilizations. First they established the Indus Saraswati rural one establishing also the first towns in it including towns like Mohenjo-daro in southern Pakistan, Harappa in the Punjab and Lothal in Gujarat.

Later with further assimilation of inputs from the north, i.e from Kangra, Taxila region, Hoshiarpur, Kashmir and distant Pamirs, the Punjabees of the plains blossomed forth into Aryan civilization. This spread first into the rest of the Indo-Gangetic plain when enriched by inputs from the Punjabees of the trans-Indus region up to the Hindu Kush mountains. Broadened further by the creative contributions of the Buddha and the Jain Tirthankers, the Hindu-Buddhist civilization and culture spread far and wide in Asia and still exists in the world as a major constituent of the world culture.

3.2 Harappan Culture

The traces of Palaeolithic stone age or the old stone age of pebble tools have been unearthed dated from 5000 to 4000 B.C. in the Sohan basin near Rawalpindi and in Kangra region or the Ban-Ganga basin of the Kalka region. These traces are covered by the strata bearing remains from the Indus-

Saraswati culture or the Harappan culture of the Punjab. The finds near Rupar date from 1400 B.C. to 200 B.C. There are many more such sites in the Saraswati area (more than a thousand) than in the Indus region (about 300) from Jhelum to Balochistan. Major finds exist in the country-side near Rupar. The whole area covered by this rural civilization is now recognized as a Punjabee village of gigantic proportions. Agriculture was the main profession. The unearthed artifacts include fishing hooks, adornment items for ladies and inscribed pottery; (the inscriptions and Harappan writing and language are still a closed book). The merchants seemed to do their book keeping in the style of the middle eastern empires, but there are claims of linguistic kinship with later Gujarati and Punjabi languages.

The archaeological excavations began in the culture's ultimate cities and trade centres like Mohenjo-daro and Lothal in the southernmost reaches of the culture and the excavations proceeded northwards where the culture had begun and matured. In the Punjab, the children still play with the type of toys baked from clay which are discovered in the buried remains of this culture. The historians now believe that this Harappan culture started from the ancient villages of the Punjab and progressed along the courses of the Punjab rivers including the ancient Saraswati course flowing from the Kalka Sivaliks into Rajasthan where it dried up. The people loved life. The excavations revealed clay chessmen in the mounds of Girdi in Hissar. Similar articles were unearthed near Thanesar, Kaithal and Rohtak. It is not incumbent that some outside agency must have destroyed this cultural upsurge. It could have gone out of stream through natural fatigue and the people having taken to newer ways like the Aryan Hindu culture that later spread from practically the same Punjabees of north and central Punjab. Such evidence comes from the cheek by jowl findings of Harappan pottery shreds and those evolved later as the Vedic pottery.

3.3 Vedic Culture

The Punjabees are credited for having created the Vedic values and the Vedic gods whose abode was imagined to be the Kailash mountain and lake Mansarovar. The change agents must have been the influx of fresh arrival of tribes from the central Himalayas and beyond from Kashmir and the Pamir area. The evolution and spread of the Hindu-Buddhist culture all over the then Asian world has been expressed earlier. It also would carry the culture of other bronze age areas of present day Pakistan, Hindu Kush region and East India. Whatever we learn of the Vedic age Punjabees and their proneness now to indulge in internal strife is from the remembered Hindu texts besides archaeology. Vyas mentions how the Mahabharata hero Krishna had been invited by the Harappans before the Mahabharata war to provide security to them by establishing himself at Dwarka in Gujarat against a feared attack from trading rivals from the Persian Gulf. Raja Virat of Hoshiarpur provided refuge to the Pandavas in their incognito exile.

The major religious texts are the Vedas among which the *Rig Veda* and the *Atharva Veda* are the principal ones giving information about the times. Some of the information given is rather visionary. Besides talking of gold ornaments and its profuse use in decorating the chariots or their heroes. There is considerable allusion to the use of rockets. The later day Puranas and Samritis are also valuable sources. The major tribes identified there are the Malwas, Yaudehas, Gujjars, Purus, Trigarta, Madre, Yavan, fighting Brahmans, Wahis, Aroras, Kamboja, Gandhara, Vratya, Sibis etc. Many more warlike tribes arose from the settlements of the foreigners in the wake of incursions by Greek, Sakas, Kushanas and Persians. These incursions reached few times from the west up to the Beas. In the distant past, Multan and Lahore became provinces of the Persian empire for extended periods. Punjabees in return often conquered parts of Iran and Afghanistan up to Hindu Kush for some Indian empire or the other that extended westwards. Pukkusati, the ruler of the Punjab in the sixth-seventh century B.C. was exchanging ambassadors with Medea and Chaldea in Iran.

In principle, the Aryan kings governed with the assent of the subjects. It was considered a kingly duty to expand the kingdom by all possible means. Inter-state relations were of armed truce and alert watchfulness. There were kaleidoscopic alliances and aggression on the weaker states. The wars were only for a king to become an emperor but not for the physical or economic serious loss to the weaker state. The wars were fought in chariots often decorated in gold. There is mention of use of simple rockets.The Punjab thus became an arena of fighters; usually the Brahmans engaged in learning and teaching in their shrines and *gurukuls* were left alone. The people of the Punjab, to start with were pastoral people engaged in raising sheep and cattle and became the earliest tillers of the land. The arts of civilization soon appeared when they had surplus of food. They developed the system of fairs, festivals and centres of pilgrimage. They were devoted to the plough and the tilling of the land. Balrama, who popularized the plough was an elder brother of Krishna the chief leader and philosopher of the Mahabharata. When the pride and behaviour of the Brahmans became unbearable, Vishwamitra and Rama incarnation of Vishnu appeared to demonstrate the poetic and religious heights attained by the Kshatriya non-Brahmans. Opposite to this there was the creation of Parshu Rama, a clear role model for fighting Brahmans for humbling the pride of the Kshatriya kings. Thus the thinkers always worked for a balance between castes.

Harappan Punjabees must have been the first to yoke oxen to the plough. They made the humped ox a sacred animal, a pet and a companion of Siva, their *pashupati* who soon was to become the chief of the Hindu gods who had their abode at mount Kailash and lake Mansarovar, and also the altars in every Hindu village. Parvati, the mother goddess of every wild tribe was given the status of the consort of Siva. Cow became first the totem of the agricultural communities and then a sacred animal of the Hindus. The Aryans called a Vedic hymn usually of four "feet" also a cow. This was the basis of allegations hurled at each other if one suppressed some hymns in his/her teaching of the Vedas. The fault was placed at the same level as the theft of a cow, a heinous offence in the agrarian world of old.

The whole of western India became a large Punjabi village in the early Harappan age. With the trading impulse of Dravidians settled also in the Punjabee village, the first urbanization started. (The Mahabharata has been assessed by certain scholars as conflict between the village and the city.) The Harappans in the lower reaches of Sindh set up village republics with an elected and popular chief known as *Karta* or the chief executive. A prominent *Karta* was Bharat. He was very innovative and decided to send a friendship expedition upstream along the Indus and get acquainted with the Hindus living around the Kabul valley close to the Hindu Kush. This again helped the joint Hindu culture to develop in the Sapta Sindhu Desh from where the Aryas in their migration eastwards along the Ganges spread Hinduism or humanism mixed with the adoration of Siva and the cow to all corners of India. In the spread of common ethical discipline the contribution of Asoka the first Hindu-Buddhist monarch was great indeed. Asoka was the grandson of Chandragupta Maurya who had established the Mauryan empire primarily with the ideology that developed around Taxila. The Mauryan empire was practically a Punjabi empire since the empire building by Chandragupta Maurya started in the Punjab with the assistance of his mentor Kautilya of Taxila University with the support from the Punjab rebels from the Greek yoke after the debacle of Porus. A Greek Buddhist kingdom lasted at Taxila till 170 B.C. Later a Rajput kingdom was established at Multan which was subsequently absorbed in the Chach and Daher dynasty of Sind that lasted till conquest of Sind by the Arabs in the eighth century A.D. The later Vedic age was ridden with conflicts between Kshatriyas and Brahmans. Individual valour was as much prized as noble lineage. If one neglected the duties enjoined on him, he could lose caste status. In the heroic age family life was very important and the wife was placed on a pedestal. Brothers could belong to different castes in the same family. Mahabharata times saw transition from tribal to professional structure of society. The river Sutlej was a dividing line socio-culturally of northern Punjab from the area around Kurukshetra. Madres of Sialkot were the leading Punjabees. Aroras were old Punjabees when Ionian mixing was found in Kambojas, Gandharas and Yavanas. There was political instability and in consequence social fluidity. Savitri was a Malwa woman. (Savitri name became a popular name in Muslim Java.) Savitri in her dialogue with death pronounced eternal religion as love and charity and absence of ill will in word, deed and thought for all living things.

3.4 Hinduism

Hinduism included the wisdom of the Buddha and of the Jain Tirthankers, and the concept of a caring god from the Hindu Kush tribes who had been exposed also to the middle eastern religions centred around victory over death through philosophical and astrological beliefs. The Punjabees polished the monotheism to include Buddhist meditation, and Hindu accent on success in worldly life (converting it later to a practical humanist and *Bhakti* religion of the Sikhs). The primitive Punjabi village society had developed cooperation in distinct farms and the Punjabees developed the arts of selfless service to fellow men. Hindu totemic symbols of bull, pipal tree and other items of flora and fauna became common. They recognized the Dravidian god Siva as master of beasts (Pashu Pati in Punjabi language), a dweller of high Himalayas (Mt. Kailash and lake Mansarovar) with his consort (Gauri – Parvati) who was the mother goddess of all wild forest dwellers. The Punjab has the Siva or Parvati temples in various names all over the hill tract from Kangra to Uttaranchal. Vaishnavism entered from the conception of a caring god because of Buddhist Mahayana that had spread to the Hindu Kush region of native Hindus who gave the name Hindu to the religion of the then Punjabees and this name stuck to the religion of all Indians, becoming identified with the Indian way of life.

Gifted individuals were inspired to compose the Vedas and epics of *Ramayana* and *Mahabharata* in the hermitages in Kashmir and the Punjab. Sanskrit grammarian Panini also was of the Punjab. In the early Vedic age considerable strife existed in the Punjab involving the Punjabees in all kinds of feuds. Each king of tiny kingdom was engaged in striving against the neighbour king. The hero was king Divodas. He and his son Sudas clashed with the clan of Bharatas and these fights on the banks of the Ravi are recorded in the Vedas. Many tribes moved south along the course of the Saraswati. The Mahabharat holocaust at Kurukshetra happened any time between 1400 B.C. to 2500 B.C. The Kuru-Panchala alliance including Krivis and Bharatas was victorious at Kurukshetra. The Rig Veda mentions also Yadus and Turvasa tribes of southern Punjab. The Matsyas lived to the south of Delhi. The Pakhtas, Vishervas and Sivas were of eastern Afghanistan. Dasas, Kiratas, Chandalas, were the tribes of the east who resisted the Aryan intruders eastward of Delhi. The Sibis lived in the Shorekot region of Jhang. The Kasis, Kosalas, Videhas became prominent only in the later Vedic age. In the Buddha's times Madres lived between the Ravi and Chenab. Panini, the Sanskrit grammarian lived at Kaithal. Ram Chandra, the hero of the Ramayana and a prince of Ayodhya was born at Ghuran few kms from Patiala.

Buddhist stupas have been uncovered near Ambala including the pillar later transplanted at Feroz Shah Kotla in Delhi. Engraved on stone, the Rattapida Sutta and Buddhist edicts have been found at Dhankot near Gurgaon and at Ambala respectively. The Buddha included Kuru Dharma of the code of Manu in his sermons.

Nagnajit, a king of Gandhara propagated the cult of the Soma drink. The Aryans loved to chant, sing and dance and indulge in chariot racing , gambling and poetic contests. They used the Veena, flute and the drums as musical instruments. The Punjabees were superstitious and feared bad luck when predicted by astrology and omens which could be overcome by fasts and charity. King Porus of the Purus consolidated his kingdom east of the Jhelum and bore the attack of Alexander who had first overcome some resistance at Mahabed on the right bank of the Indus in the present Yusufzai tribal country. Historic times started with the sermons of the Buddha who travelled and gave sermons in the Punjab at least twice in his life time.

From the study of coins discovered in various places in the Punjab, it is evident that Greek technology was adopted by some Indian states, particularly in minting their coinage and better sculpture as is evident from the development of Gandhara and Mathura schools of art and sculpture. Some Hindu-Buddhist Greek soldiers set up independent principalities in the Punjab which lasted about five centuries after the Alexander's return to Iran where soon afterwards he died on account of wounds and strain of the Indian expedition. He was blocked from going further east beyond Beas in the Punjab and he returned by a more hazardous but shorter route than the one he had taken to come this far. Since then a good proportion of Punjabees had a Greek-Persian strain in them particularly since Partheans and Medeans now migrated to India in the wake of fresh incursions of Huns, Scythians and Turkish tribes professing Hindu-Buddhism.

3.5 Harappan Sites Unearthed in India

Kotla Nidag, Rupar	200 B.C. to 1400 B.C.
Bara	8 km south of Rupar
Dhang	19 km from Rupar
Mehranwala	26 km from Nalagarh
Sanghol	Midway on Chandigarh-Ludhiana Road

Sanghol lies on the large buried Buddhist monastery and large town of that name where Hieun Tsang stayed many days on his travel across the Punjab. There is an archaeology museum also at Sanghol where the base of a large Stupa has been discovered.

Abadiala Kalan	29 km south east of Ludhiana
Rekhi Brarh	11 km south of Jind
Raja Sirkap Late Harappan site	3 km south of Faridkot
Daulatpur	5 km from Thanesar
Mita Thal	near Chandigarh
Dera Ghazi Khan and near Mianwali	(Bannu region)
Phillaur	near Jalandhar
Kangra District	near Nurpur
Girdi and Kunal	Hissar (Chessmen of Harrapan times also found)
Changal Dhera (Mardan District)	Buddhist stupa and railing

3.6 Other Important Prehistoric Sites

Tilla near Jhelum	reputed samadhi of Raja Bhartari Hari who died after turning into a jogi on discovering the infidelity of his beloved queen.
Hoshiarpur is reputed to be on the site of Raja Virat's capital city where the	Pandavas spent their stipulated one year of incognito exile.
Dholbaha (Hoshiarpur)	Excavations have unearthed industrial scale production of idols and pottery toys.
Kurukshetra-Thanesar region	Many sites and monuments relating to the Mahabharata Age. Excavations at Karan Ka Qila cover 2000 B.C. to 500 A.D.
Rohtak	Certain sites depict Brahmi and Kharoshthi scripts. Mauryan coins also discovered.
Delhi	Feroz Shah Kotla pillar excavated from Ambala is inscribed with Buddhist edicts.

A site near Malot	Ruins of a large Hindu Shahi period temple.
Mardan District (Pakistan)	Buddhist ruins at village Changal Dhera (old bricks of size 21x10x3 cm.)
Sehwan, Kafir Qila (on the road to Malot, Pakistan)	Ruins of an ancient temple.
Adi Badri (Yamuna Nagar District)	An ancient pilgrim stop-over on the ancient route to Badri Nath and beyond to Tibet. This is where the mythical river Saraswati entered Haryana.

(Ancient coins indicate that the Naukhari kings of the Punjab waged wars with the Huns ruling as Buddhists in Kabul and Kapisa confining them to the territory beyond the Indus. Coins discovered at Mathura and Gurgaon were minted by a Mahakshatrapa appointee of the Mauryan empire.)

3.7 More Pre-History (recorded by Greek and Persian scholars of old)

Kuru and Puru Janpeeths (republics) existed in the Punjab in the sixth century B.C. Harshvardhan belonged to the Shrikanth Janpeeth of Thanesar. He later became an emperor at Kanauj. Kuru country was known to be the land of warriors. They believed in Kuru Riti, the moral code practically adopted by the Buddha. Kuru Kshetra was a pilgrim town from ancient times. It was sacked by Nadir Shah in 1739 after he had looted Delhi. Pakkusati ruled Punjab from Kangra but his dynasty lasted only till 515 B.C. King Pakkusati had sent an embassy to the king of Medea. And had collected a loan taken earlier by Cyrus the great for his wars in the north. Darius of Persia conquered Kapisa and extended his empire to the Indus. Greek Buddhist colonies flourished in Kapisa and at Bhera in the Punjab. Small Buddhist kingdoms existed few centuries after the debacle of Porus who was killed by conspiracies begun by Chanakya the minister of Chandragupta Maurya. Sibis and Pauravas ruled the doab between the Chenab and the Jhelum rivers. The Sibis had their capital at Shivpuri. Later half of the second century B.C. saw a back and forth struggle between the Sakas, Kushans (all professing Hindu-Buddhism) and remnants of

Greek (Hindu-Buddhist) kingdoms. From internal and external evidence the Mahabharata war could have occurred some time between 1400 B.C. and 2400 B.C. according to different authorities from the possible genealogies of some dated individuals like the king Milinda of the Buddhist texts.

This was the period when the Punjabees started amassing private property. Peasants were allotted land in perpetuity and trade flourished, migration to foreign lands became a passion of the Punjabees. The first giant Buddha statue was carved at Bamian marking the portals of Hindu-Buddhist lands to the east. Buddhism was to carry the influence of Greek thinking. The Buddhists regard the period from the Bactrian Greeks to the inroads of Huns from Tibet as the period of decline of religion. Tribes of Haryana fought patriotic wars against the powerful Sakas and Kushans or Huns from distant lands or from Tibet. There was revival of Hinduism and Sanskrit in the Punjab. Heroic tradition of the Punjabees was strengthened both by fables and by actions. The Buddhist saga of raja Sibi of Charsadda who fed an eagle from his own body as compensation for rescuing a dove from his claws is one such fable. Yaudehas led the fight against Kushans whose empire covered most of west Asia with their capital at Peshawar. Punjab became the sword arm of India second time after Kautalya. When Heun Tsang visited the Punjab during his return journey to China, only Multan flourished as an Indo-Greek Buddhist state. Lahore was a Hindu Shahi town till 999 A.D. The fate tilted against the Punjabi kingdoms when a confederacy put together by Anand Pal was defeated through lack of proper communication among the confederates in the battle at Peshawer and the single command of Mahmood prevailed for the victory of the invading Islam.

The heroism of the Punjabees always showed up cracks in advanced planning and preparation. Only warfare of dispersed leadership of the Sikh Misls could harness it properly to show results.

4 PUNJAB, ARENA FOR EMPIRES

4.1 After 323 B.C.

Alexander had invaded India after his conquest of the Persian empire. His armies crossed Indus at Jhelum and defeated Porus in a bloody battle but won over Porus to be his ally and to continue to rule in his name. Alexander advanced to Beas but his army was disheartened by the continued opposition to the advance and the bloody battles Alexander had to wage with the disputing Malls of Multan in order to secure his retreat. They had also listened to the rumours of a powerful king in the east of India with much larger army with war elephants than that of Porus. When the army was reluctant to advance further into India, Alexander was forced to retreat along the southern route and reached Iran from across Balochistan. He was also wounded in battle but he managed to reach his Persian capital in 323 B.C. where he died. The present Pakistan territory came into the possession of west Asian authorities succeeding Alexander. The patriotic faculty at Taxila Hindu-Buddhist University included a genius Chanakya who had also got a warrior disciple Chandragupta Maurya whom he had handpicked. He was the unrecognized son of the Nanda king of Pataliputra from a Punjabi mother Mura. The Taxila intellectuals and Chandragupta Maurya carried on a successful uprising against the imposed Greek-Persian over-lords of the Punjab. Porus was killed in an ambush. Chanakya, the master conspirator made alliance with certain disgruntled ministers of the Nanda king in the name of the unrecognized son of the king. The conspiracy was successful and soon Maurya became the king with Chanakya as the chief minister at Pataliputra.

The successor to Alexander's authority for his Indian possessions was Seleucus with his seat of Authority in Central Asia. He made a bid to take control and attacked across the Indus but was roundly defeated and agreed to a humiliating peace, marrying his daughter to the Indian emperor. His ambassador Magasthnese stationed at the Pataliputra court has written a glowing account of peace and prosperity in India and of the architecture of Pataliputra.(The ancient Pataliputra in part is still visible from above, where it lies sunk in a lake sized tank in Patna). Asoka was the grandson of Chandragupta Maurya. After winning a bloody battle with Kalinga, he got a revulsion against war and became a Buddhist. He was convinced that the Buddha's teaching will be good for the public of all lands. He sent embassies and preachers to many foreign countries including Sri Lanka where he sent his daughter to set up a Buddhist Sangha, an authority and refuge for the followers of the Buddha. A sapling of the *pipal* tree at Gaya, sitting under which Buddha gained enlightenment, was planted in Sri Lanka and through the devout attention received there it is flourishing in successive offsprings. Asoka caused his edicts about the religious duty (Dhamma) of the people to be engraved in stone or on stupas planted all over his empire and on the routes to distant lands. A stupa has been transplanted in Delhi at Feroz Shah Kotla and an edict engraved on a rock is placed at the entrance of the National Museum at Delhi. It is estimated that more than 2000 engraved edicts were scattered around India and now and then are discovered. Some pockets of Greeks and Scythians settled in India as Hindus, but their rule at Rawalpindi was overthrown by the Punjabi Yadavas. The Scythian or Kushan settlers were Kshatriyas from distant Georgia with last names borrowed from the rivers and natural features of Georgia. Such names can be recognized as many Khatri caste names of the Punjabees.

4.2 Buddhism in the Punjab

The Buddha decentralized the acquisition of highest wisdom to the level of the individual. The individualistic Punjabees would naturally be attracted to his teaching. Their holy books, i.e. the Vedas had already given hints about ethics and morality being natural to human beings without any supernatural props. Jainism and Buddhism, the philosophies, having no need of belief in an omnipresent and all controlling deity and then tying themselves in knots squaring the mundane world with the existence of such a super humanistic deity, spread all over the Punjab. The springs of Jainism happened to exist (native places of the twenty-four Tirthankers) outside the Punjab. The Jain monks and nuns constituted a new aspect of religious asceticism. Their insistence on vegetarianism grounded Jainism to India away from partakers of fish and fowl. The Jainism flourished in the south-east of the Punjab around Rohtak, Hissar, Agra and Delhi. Many Jain temples and some evidence of ancient monasteries exist in this region besides others in the east and the south. Many cave shelters were first occupied by the Jains and later expanded by the Hindu-Buddhists; these now constitute the wonders of ancient and medieval India like the Ajanta and ellora caves or caves around Nasik, or in Orissa and in Nagarjunkonda. The Buddhist records warrant that the Buddha personally visited the flock in the Punjab atleast twice in his life time. Since both Asoka and Kanishka identified themselves as Buddhists, the Buddhist teaching became widespread also in the Punjab. The Punjab was close to major Buddhist centres of art and learning like Sanchi, Mathura, Sanghol, Taxila and Gandhara. The Humanism and secularism, the religion of the Punjabees was strengthened by both Jainism and Buddhism. The empire of Kanishka spread mostly westwards from Taxila and Peshawer, but the centres of the Buddhist learning were extending from Taxila and Srinagar in Kashmir, to Attock, Sialkot and Sanghol to Mathura and Varanasi. The archaeologists have unearthed many monuments in the Punjab notably at Taxila and Sanghol. Many sites of Asokan carved rock edicts and Buddhist stupas have been identified in the extended Punjab of that day.

There seems to be an identifiable influence of the Punjabi mind on the Buddha when he must have travelled as an ascetic, before his enlightenment, in the Kuru country around Delhi. The area was under the influence of the Jain ideology centred around mental faculties allegedly sharpened by denial of the material body and the ancient beliefs (of the Hindu Sanatan Dharma) in natural humanism of kindness and trust. The Kurus had already adopted a code of ethics known as the Kuru code for civilized behaviour which had travelled far and wide due to the popularity of Kurukshetra as a focus of pilgrimage besides the famous places along the Ganges or in the High Himalayas. The Buddha seems to have given a sermon at Kurukshetra after his enlightenment.

The Punjabees were active both as pilgrims and traders along the silk route to China, a branch of which passed through Bamian west of Hindukush and another through Kabul, Mansehra and Murree to Samarkand. Many Buddhist teachers and preachers travelled from the Punjab and Kashmir to Chinese Turkistan and beyond. Whole of Asia had become a common market. Indian diaspora including Punjabees travelled to many foreign countries and settled there. There is a record in China of an Indian merchant voyaging with them to distant South America. The world was pretty much borderless in those days of tolerance and ascendance of central Asian piety.

In the post-modern world, Indians are again welcome in most countries for the expected talent or for proneness to peaceful hard work whether of opening up of backward interiors, or taming the harsh soil for agricultural abundance or for teaching languages, literature or arithmetic. There are many Punjabees in the international peace keeping and development role in present times too.

4.3 Punjab after the Buddhist Empires

Kanishka's Buddhist-Kushan empire sheltered the Punjab from expansionist Persians for few centuries. The empires tend to expand into a power vacuum. The Chinese empire nibbled at Mongolia and Tibet but stopped short of Russia in the north and the Japanese and British power to the East and the South. The Mughal and the British empires in India became restricted to India because of jealousies of other world powers and continued internal strife. The Persian power had not collapsed from defeat. Alexander himself became a Persian emperor and the Greeks tried to maintain Greek-Persian hold over new kingdoms of central Asia. The Kushan-Indian empire only had skirted the major areas of Greek-Persian power. And after few emperors at Peshawar, the Kanishka empire broke into many parts. The Hinduized Sakas and Kushans established small kingdoms in parts of the Punjab and other parts of India. Certain compact groups set up caste republics giving name to many Kshatriya castes derived from the names of distant Georgian natural features and rivers. The Punjab and Haryana *jats, certain aroras and agarwal* subcastes, possibly of similar extraction, showed their warlike prowess in continued occupation of their chosen areas around Delhi, in Haryana as well as in Uttar Pradesh; they provided the muscle to the surviving Jains and Buddhists. The Buddhist philosophy became absorbed fully in Hinduism but showed up particularly in the beliefs of the Sikhs and the Sufis of the Punjab, who in principle followed the religions of theistic devotion (*bhakti*), not only of God, but also of the preceptor (*the guru or the pir*).

What little is known about interregnum period between

the Mauryan empire and the Gupta empire about the conditions in the Punjab, is learnt from the finding of the ancient coins and inscriptions from the diggings or from the possession of individuals with some connection with temples and old monasteries or from records of travellers of old. Megasthnese has mentioned the nomad shepherds and graziers of cattle of the Punjab. They exist even now. The tribes with Naga totems or the ancient Nagas lived in the hills and forests of the sub-mountainous region. The celebration of *Nag-panchmi* continues from Vedic times in the Beas valley. After the Roman trade contacts and Greek connection, Indian rulers began striking their own coins. Sculpture also got a lift. Gandhar was ruled by a Buddhist ruler Virsena in 225 B.C. and by Bactrian ruler in 185 B.C. and his successors. A king famous in Buddhist legends, Menander in Greek or king Milinda of Buddhist literature ruled Punjab from Sialkot up to 110 B.C. Raja Salivahan of Sialkot expanded his realm up to Multan and further south to Sind. Huns had a minor foray into India and had occupied Taxila, but were expelled by a Parthian force. Kushans were Hindu-Buddhists and favoured Manichean tolerant attitude of Mahayana Buddhism. Kushan Buddhist empire (capital Peshawer) extended from Taxila to the Caspian sea.

Asokan inscriptions in Mansehra and on stupas near Rawalpindi and Bahawalpur indicate the widespread inclusion of Buddhist teaching in the Punjab. There are ruins of a temple near Dholbaha (Hoshiarpur) from 200 A.D. and ruins of a monastery near Bathinda from the same period. Soon after there was a revulsion against all foreign rulers who had established their own Hindu-Buddhist kingdoms in India. The Punjabees were in the fore-front of such resistence spreading from Malwa and Ajmer to centres at Bathinda, Kurukshetra, Thanesar or Multan and beyond west-wards. We have deliberately used the compound word Hindu-Buddhist from the certainty that there is Indian cultural base of the continuous spectrum of Punjabee beliefs from Sanatan

Dharma of the Hindus to their perception by the Buddhists and there was a constant interplay between various philosophies. Sakas and Kushans could be overthrown from power seats in India only by militant Hinduism resulting in the rise to imperial power of the Guptas, Raja Bikramajit of Ujjain and Harshvardhan of Thanesar and later of Kanauj. The centres of their power were outside the Punjab. The victory of Raja of Kanauj at Kasur in 550 A.D. cleared India of Huns and Kushanas.

Trade with the Roman empire brought in wealth and progress in art and sculpture. There was export of iron and metal ware and jewellery. The Hun, Saka and Kushan regimes when not popular were overthrown by the subjects. The prominent Punjabee warriors in these struggles were the Yaudehas, and Kunundas. Buddhism and Brahmanism coexisted. According to Chinese and Korean travellers, the Punjabees were productive, philanthropic and humane. They abhorred deceit and were keen to fulfil their obligations.

4.4 Golden Age of India

The Buddhist empires were vertically split between the laity and the celibate monks and nuns of the Sangha made supreme by Buddha's desire. The arts and crafts flourished and trade became galvanized by borderless Asia and honest dealings of Indian merchants. The professions involving violence as fighting or fishing languished. There were the beginnings of golden age of Indian culture not only in India but also its transplants in Cambodia, Java and Samarquand. The Gupta power first acquired Pataliputra and Magadha and later reached out to extend the Gupta empire across India from Assam to the Punjab. The Persian empire extended in the east to Lahore and Multan, but had Hindu Buddhist Greeks and Afghans as governors who as the Indian power grew in the east and when there was any opportunity became independent rulers of small kingdoms. The chief such kingdoms were of Sialkot allied to Kashmir and of Kabul allied to that of Taxila. The flow of pilgrims to the Punjab and to the Punjabi Buddhist and Jain monasteries had prosperous times as vouchsafed by the Chinese travellers Fa-Hien of the fourth century A.D. and Yuan Chwang of the seventh century A.D. towards the beginning and the end of the "golden age". The golden age had a critical time when under Mehergul, a branch of the Huns shook the Gupta empire to its roots, but the golden age was rescued by the Punjabi ruler Harsh Vardhan of Thanesar, who under Hindu revivalist banner threw out the Huns from the Punjab and Malwa and changed his capital city to the imperial city of Kanauj. The prosperity of India at the close of the golden age can be assessed from the reported existence of ten thousand temples in Kanauj, the capital city alone, which the Moslem invaders destroyed in the 11th century when they raided and looted it. As a crowning glory of the golden age, the Chinese traveller was witness to the quinquennial celebration of the birthday of Harsh when he emptied his entire treasury in charity to religious and other interests of his subjects. He even divested himself of his royal garments and regalia for charity. He displayed that the state amassed wealth for the subjects.

4.5 The Hindu Shahis of Kabul

The Shahis, a Hindu dynasty of Kabul was very powerful. They stood guard against the Arab-Iranian combine during the first Muslim expansion into Asia from the eighth to the tenth century A.D. A Buddhist branch of the Shahis controlled western Afghanistan beyond the Hindu Kush from 475 A.D. The Hindu-Buddhist scholars and scientists flourished in the Punjab during this period. They produced the current version of the *Ramayana* and the *Mahabharata*. The Shahis had started as underlings of the Tibetan Huns in power in both eastern and western Afghanistan and had been elevated with the Tibetan title "Shah" and when the Huns became weak, the Shahis assumed royal powers as well as became staunch allies of Kashmir Rajas. They built a second capital at Udbhangpura to which they shifted when eventually Kabul was lost to the Arab-Iranian armies. The first Shahi ruler at Zabol used the Tibetan title Tegin. A Tegin was ruling in the Tochi valley in the ninth century A.D. The Tegins had opposed expansion of Kanauj empire in 605 A.D. The Huns had first succeeded in expelling Hinduized Scythians from seats of power in the Persian empire in India. They expelled the Taxila ruler to take refuge at Sialkot. The white Huns established a kingdom at Kapisa (Zabul) and one at Kabul which became independent Hindu- Buddhist Shahi kingdoms. The Shahis had to wage a struggle with the Tibetan Tegin of Gandhara. The golden age of India had a critical time when under Mehergul, a branch of the Huns, attacked the Gupta empire but it was rescued by the ruler of Thanesar who became the emperor Harsh Vardhan at Kanauj. As mentioned earlier the Huns were subdued by the imperial Guptas later at Kasur. The Hun remnants were expelled from Sialkot by the Punjabees of Scythian descent in 545 A.D. Salivahan and Rasalu were the hero kings of Sialkot. The Punjabi bards still sing about their deeds.

4.6 Some Historical Events

Torman and his son Mehergul, two white Hun rulers of Sialkot, practiced their wonted cruelty on Buddhists and almost eliminated their monasteries and monks from the Punjab. Centuries earlier Bikramajit I of Ujjain had expelled the Sakas from Malwa when he started his Indian Bikrami era in about 70 A.D. In the last quarter of the fourth century A.D., Samudra Gupta, the ruler of Kanauj occupied Kurukshetra but later king Lalitaditya of Kashmir wrested its control. Harsh Vardhan became the head of the Srikantha Janpad of Thanesar at the young age of sixteen in 606 A.D. He was a Saivite and soon set about expelling Sakas and Kushans who were nibbling at the Gupta empire weakened by the struggle against the Huns. Taki near Wazirabad of Punjab (P) was the Punjab capital in 633 A.D. Great temples existed at Multan, Nurpur, Lahore, Kangra, Thanesar, Pehova, Kurukshetra, and Chamba. King Lalitaditya of Kashmir had erected a temple of Brahma at Martand, perhaps an only such temple. Martand was significant as an objective of loot that delayed the tribals in their race to seize Srinagar in the first Pakistani aggression just after their independence in 1947.

Around 700 A.D., the Shahi king of Kabul halted the first Arab Iranian attack on Kabul. Raja Rasalu the prince of Sialkot killed the ruler of Attock in single combat, who was an ally of the Arabs. In 986-87 A.D. the Turkish Sultan Subkatgin invaded Punjab but was repulsed by Jaipal of Bathinda. The Ghaznavids kept up their annual attacks in search of loot and captives. Delhi was a Rajput city in 903 A.D. After the defeat of Prithvi Raj Chauhan of Ajmer at the hands of Mohammed Ghauri in the second battle of Tarain in 1192, the Delhi Sultanate was established with continuous inputs of Moslem Jehadi forces from across the Indus and the dark days of Punjab history began soaked in the slaughter of the Hindus trying to save their temple towns and splendid forts against better armed and united adversaries pouring in from the vast stretches of Asia. The Ghaznavids had held Kurukshetra for some time but it was soon liberated. It was however spared by Sikander Lodhi due to regard for the sentiments of his Hindu subjects as pointed out to him by a Muslim religious adviser. When Akbar visited the solar eclipse fair there, he noticed the usual argument between various Sanysins and Jogis regarding the right of precedence for the holy dip! The eclipses were fully understood by the Hindu astronomers, yet they allowed the astrologers propagate superstitious beliefs since that led to large sums in charity reaching the Brahmans as well as promoted liberal charity to the poor.

With the establishment of the Delhi sultanate, a new chapter of history began for the entire country.

4.7 The Present Day Punjabees

It is a most difficult question for any historian unless the simplistic answer suffices. Punjabees are those who can demonstrate their domicile to be in the Punjab. A Punjabee living outside the Punjab has to have a sustainable claim that his ancestor due to some reason or the other shifted out from the Punjab after residing in the Punjab and he should have some fluency in the spoken Punjabi language. Such a Punjabee could be a descendent of an ancient Punjabee or an ancient fief holder or one having land rights bestowed by some Punjab ruler or victorious invader/immigrant/ occupant in the wake of some infiltrating landless immigrants trying their luck in the hospitable barren and jungle or bush clad land inside Punjab. Many times during eclipse of kings ruling over Punjab region, the borders that were always ill defined could not be protected against infiltration or a small scale attack by a whole migrating group. Such a Punjabee could also show his descent from a religious elevated person who used to be established in some Punjab village on the strength of his piety, local service or service in some religious position like attending to the upkeep of a shrine or a tomb or a village water source.

The ancient descent for modern Punjabee can be categorized as follows :

(a) Natives of the Punjab since the days of Asoka's rule, or those that claimed to have their ancestors come to the Punjab during the Mahabharata war, or those that had ancestors who had heard the Buddha or the Jain saints preach in the Punjab, or those that had ancestors who were allotted land rights by victorious Sakas, Kushans, or the Ghaznavids and Delhi sultans and kings or their representatives.

(b) Progeny of peaceful as well as aggressive Baluch tribes who migrated *en masse* on account of acute land hunger in their barren heights and migrated northwards along both sides of the Indus river and would usually settle in the Punjab up to Multan after the establishment of the Arab Caliphate in Baghdad. They came in conflict with Hindu Buddhist rulers on both sides of the Indus river. Aggressive Baluchi immigration occurred particularly after the collapse of the Mughal empire which had adequate border protection system in alliance with local fiefdoms. Jats had also infiltrated into the Punjab from Tashkent much earlier.

(c) Members of peaceful as well as aggressive Rajput and Jat groups and individuals going across the Delhi region to greener pastures in Northern Punjab and Himachal region. Most rulers and *jagirdars* of northern Punjab and Punjab hill states were Rajputs and had to establish their authority. Some had been humbled in their native lands, but some were reaping rewards of military service to various Sultans and war lords. Ultimately after the collapse of the Mughal overlordship, some had to surrender their fiefdoms to the Sikh Misls or to Maharaja Ranjit Singh. The British after the 1857 mutiny reinstated whatever had been settled by Maharaja Ranjit Singh.

(d) Muslim followers chiefly of Sufi persuasion came to the Punjab in hordes but were soon sent forward to Bengal by the Sunni rulers. The Shias preferred to go on to U.P., though some stayed behind in the Punjab. Muslims of Sunni persuasion regarded India to be perpetually in need of Afghan and Persian support for bolstering the shaky Muslim rule during dynasty changes at Delhi though it was buttressed later by an imperial alliance with the Rajputs. The Afghans (Sunni Muslims) regarded Sirhind and Bassi Pathanan near Chandigarh as their holy land second to Arabia. The Afghans could not make a deal with

Akbar and Akbar actually invaded and annexed Afghanistan to his empire. The Afghans energetically supported the Mughal sovereignty over the Punjab against the Marathas and the rebellious Sikhs. The Sikhs unlike the Marathas did not fight for loot but fought to get rid of tyrannical rule of the Mughal governors or Afghan warlords entrenched in Sirhind. To save the Afghan governors of Sirhind and Lahore, Ahmad Shah Abdali waged relentless wars against the Indian Punjab rebels and the Marathas who were in control of the Mughal emperor. Abdali fought the Marathas to smithereens but did not think much of the menace of the Sikhs who professed to be his agents in the Punjab. The result was total destruction of Mughal and Afghan power in the Punjab and also the demise of the imperial ambitions of the Marathas.

(c) Soon Punjab became the possession solely of Maharaja Ranjit Singh who had won the willing or unwilling submission, village after village of the entire Punjab then controlled by many Sikh Misls or independent dispersed Sikh fighting groups. The other power in India was that of the East India Company. The condition of the Punjab after the mutiny in Delhi in 1857 throws considerable light on the antecedents of the present Punjabees. After the failure of the 1857 uprising, there was complete devastation up to about 200 kms. around Delhi and Agra. After the Anglo-Sikh wars which soon followed, the whole of Punjab came under the heel of the British. The British managed to forge an alliance with the rump of the Sikh leadership with whose help they had won a victory over the mutineers and then over the Sikh empire. For the remaining period of the British rule over the Punjab, the Sikhs were helped to spread over the whole of the Punjab but India would not yet develop true nationalism and got enmeshed in the broken promises of the British. The Punjab's prosperity by the grace of the British suddenly had a terrible jolt in Punjab riots on the eve of Indian independence directly resulting from the caricature of democracy introduced by the British. India has yet to recover fully from it. One realizes that the idea of an Indian nation only existed with the Mughal kings of India, and particularly with Aurangzeb but he expected only Muslims to be in charge, forgetting the alliance and obedience of many non-Muslims to Mughal kings.

With the reorganization of the states of India, the main Punjabi states are Punjab, Haryana and Delhi. The followers of ancient Hindu Sanatan Dharma or the common Hindus of Punjab are deemed to be non-Sikhs as they do not wear long hair, though when they were given a choice, they *en masse* recorded themselves as Sikhs. The Sikhs were cut away from Hindu moorings deliberately by Sikh leadership of post-partition days fearing that Sikhs might lose a share of their well earned special rights under the regime of communal reservations started by the British. Once true democracy takes root in the country and there is universal prosperity and employment, the current mushrooming political problems of reservations of all kinds can be overcome only by summarily dismissing all elements of reservations intruding into merit criteria. However, the nation must nourish merit in every village and town in all sections of the people. This is the historical necessity for India.

5 PUNJAB UNDER ISLAMIC DESPOTS AT DELHI

5.1 Introduction

It must be fully understood that we are writing about an age when the concepts of nations or nationalism did not exist. At most there was patriotism for the village and all loyalty was to the feudal lord or the kinglet who either owned the parcel of land or had been granted the right to till it. The king had all the right to wage war on a nighbouring king and to expand own kingdom. In victory they made merry with enemy property including their women, annexed whole or part of the enemy kingdom, but soon, ...after new.... pecking order had been achieved, the usual life went on its normal merry-go-round. When the battling factions were both with same cultural values, no harm was done to each other's way of life. But when the lust for expansion was mixed with a religious urge and when the superiority of own faith was proven by force of arms, the damage to the defeated was much more severe. Rakshasas and Daityas lost their right to exist when Aryan kings expanded their hold on India. When Prithvi Raj won a victory over the neighbouring ruler of Ghaur (Afghanistan) his values were ethical and humanist, but when Ghaznavi or Ghauri committed aggression for loot or land, their values were Quranic which seemed to sanction snatching of wealth, women or land of non-Muslim enemy or at least to interfere with their worship of idols in their temples. It was callous self-glorification that allowed gross ignorance among Hindus of the nature of Islam that had already spread from Spain to Iran. Indians had only seen Muslim traders and sailors who were usually having the same values as Hindu traders and were not abreast of events that had turned the rest of the civilized world upside down all over the old Roman or the Iranian empires. Every nation has to keep abreast of the urges that prevail in the potential enemy of the neighbourhood. Since free India knew so much about Pakistan, it had to go nuclear against their best instincts which yearned for international amity and universal disarmament. When a king decided to attack a neighbour, the greed of the victorious made no distinction when sequestering the property of the enemy, Hindu or Muslim. In 1241, the invading Mughals sacked Lahore, the possession of Afghan king of Delhi. A king Hamir Dev of Kohistan in the Punjab helped Delhi in expelling the Mughals and in return was confirmed as king of Kohistan by the Muslim king of Delhi.

Prithvi Raj was over confident relying on the bravery of his soldiers and did not form any strategy for victory over his foe even after defeating him at Naraina near Kaithal in 1191. Mohammed Ghauri made a non-interference treaty with king of Kashmir and made a deal with Jai Chand of Kanauj just before he moved against Delhi (battle of Tarain) in 1192 A.D. Such state-craft by an Indian leader was only shown by Prime Minister Indira Gandhi when she managed to sign a treaty of peace and friendship with the Soviet Union just before launching her open support to Bangladesh liberation forces with massive employment of all arms.

5.2 Atrocities and Modus Vivendi

The victory and the establishment of Delhi Sultanate in 1226 A.D. was the culmination of a bloody strife extending over two centuries and had become almost a blood feud among warlike Punjabees between armies of non-Muslim Punjab rulers and Muslim rulers already established in the Punjab or those across the Indus. For centuries the Hindu-Buddhist rulers of Kashmir, Punjab and Afghanistan and beyond had controlled the land trade routes leading to China and the countries of the Iranian plateau, namely Iran and Iraq in particular. Now these countries had a chance with the establishment of the Muslim Caliphate at Baghdad. They already were exploiting the sea route through the Persian Gulf and further hop-stop to the east. The atrocities committed by the victorious armies particularly to extract wealth from the rich losers were frightful, especially the deliberate destruction of sacred objects and pilferage of all precious articles. Many women and beasts of burden were forcibly taken away. They found vast under-populated or virgin lands inviting immigration and hordes of Balochies followed, who form now the major segment of Punjabees in Pakistan. The destruction of non-Muslim power around Delhi opened the way for Muslim penetration into rest of India and conversely many Rajputs and Jats already seeking better pastures turned north reaching Punjab hill states or the Himachal river valleys along with new allottees of jagirs. The Muslim armies did not bring women or peasants and they had to avail of the locals. The new landed aristocracy was now Muslim. The non-Muslims from their skills and habits of simple living had to buy mortgage on their sequestered land since the Muslim *zamindars* very often were in debt to them. Already the Muslims were living in countries which were not ruled by them and they found an easy *modus vivendi* with the other Hindu citizens. Where the ruler was too much under the thumb of Muslim ulema, even discriminatory Jazia tax was imposed on them which was abolished only when Sikhs wrenched local control of the Punjab from them. The caste system encouraged compartmentalized social interactions and Muslims could easily have a separate niche, even though Islam frowned on caste distinction among Muslims, but caste crept in some form or the other. The neo-Muslims were a lower caste than those who claimed some Iranian or Arab ancestors. Apart from feudal and caste exploitation the village machine ran smoothly as of fore. Non-Muslims took to trade and business or to higher order technical skills. The services of the untouchables continued as before except among Muslims, the prayer in the mosque was open to all but the Muslims were kept at an arms length by Hindus in view of the remembered abhorance of the Muslim iconoclasm. Though all symbols of wealth had vanished from Hindu temples, yet the temples continued to function and the Hindus could freely attend to their customs and prayers. There was harmony between Hindu and Muslim god fearing souls.

Punjabees benefited from the rule of law enforced by the *panchayats* and Muslim *qazis*. The purse strings of all kings and their courts were controlled by the Hindus. Muslim superstitions supplemented the indigenous ones. The courts treated Hindu *Vaids* and *Unani Hakims* equally. Scientific advancement was at a fullstop, but technology improvements continued utilizing the imported skills from particularly Iran, Iraq or the rest of India.

5.3 Native Hindus of the Punjab

At that period of history, the Hindus of the Punjab were the chastised remnants of the ancient Punjabees. The Brahmans continued on their course of being the wise-heads for the villagers and kept up their convictions and riruals. The Khatris took to alternative professions or migrated to the new feudal chiefs where they could be safer. Up to the world war at least one Hindu family survived in each village in all Muslim lands of west Asia.

The Punjabi Hindus settled down to live with sprinkling of Muslims in the villages building new myths. They sang about Guga Pir, Dulo Bhatti-wala, Puran Bhagat, or Raja Rasalu who had killed in single combat the Muslim king of Attock to remove a bottleneck in the peaceful travel of Punjabees to and fro across the river Indus. Many a pious

Muslim desired to settle in the sparsely populated regions of the Punjab. The relatively even tenor was disturbed when fresh attacks started by the Mughals following the Hun explosion from Tibet. More migrants from West Asia and Central Asia started pouring into India either as prospective soldiers in the armies of Muslim expansion in India or as pious Muslims often of Sufi inclination to spread Islam in India. The peaceful interaction between Sufis and Hindus led to the recognition of Guru Nanak as a sufi saint by the Muslims and by the Hindus as a promised redeemer of the people in line with the prediction of the *Gita* that when people are in dire distress God comes as a redeemer. The violent repression of the Sikhs or the disciples of the Gurus converted the Punjabees into war-like defenders of the Punjab.

5.4 Religious Conversion

Hindus did not consider religious conversion of any importance. Every Hindu had the right and opportunity to develop spiritually and accept or change his favourite god whom he would prefer to pray. Left to merits of the case and caste restrictions prevalent among the Hindus, many might have become Muslims by choice and some did so, but the bloody conquest and initial tyranny experienced by them at the hands of victorious armies of despotic Muslim kings repelled them and they on the whole kept aloof. The Buddhist subjects had welcomed the liberation from the rule of Daher, a stickler for caste and Brahman supremacy, but when they saw the atrocities and forced conversions by the Arabs, they were repelled and sought re-admission into the Hindu system of freedom of belief. This was one case where the Hindu religious leaders allowed such re-admission and the conversion to Islam did not travel further. The Arabs after securing their coastal trade, did not pursue any adventures against other Hindu rulers. They had only once violated the state boundaries of Mewar but were roundly beaten back and the Caliph undertook never again to meddle in other Indian states and the Arabs fulfilled their promise. Another instance of Hindus sticking to the impositions of their Varanasi interpreters of *Dharma Granths* is in their refusal to allow reconversion of Kashmiri Muslims when the Dogra ruler was expanding his state under passive encouragement of the British over-lords. The Kashmir Muslims were already under the spell of Muslim Rishis of Kashmir started by Nur-ud-din Chishti whose Sufi interpretation of Islam came very close to Hindu devotion to God. The current plight of Kashmir Pandits is due to the spread of communal virus later, much after the partition of India. The hatred was fuelled by the infiltration by foreign and Pakistani terrorists in Kashmir.

Conversion and agitation against it really started with the efforts of Christian missionaries after the spread of the rule of the East India Company. The Indians protested as well as eulogized the contribution to the renaissance of Indian culture and awakening of their yearning for complete independence. The issue of conversion within established religions of India became a live issue only after the British masterful play of the communal award and planting of the poisonous seeds of fractured, religious label based democracy. The easy choice of one's religious faith and practice among the Hindus also became difficult. The Arya Samaj started a *shuddhi* movement in protest against the age old belief that one is born a Hindu and not become a member of the Hindu community by choice or by favour. As a reprisal the Muslims had their *tabligh* efforts. Sikhs also wanted to add to their numbers, but wanted only Sikhs that must display the five symbols of the Khalsa as prescribed. They in fact cut down the number of Sikhs by the elimination of those who were not agreeing to carry the required identification and the Sikh spokesmen wanted no distinction between the Sikhs and the Khalsa and incidentally wanted the Sahajdhari Sikhs to be kept away from the preferential religion based democracy coming to the Sikhs under the dispensation of the British ever grateful for Sikh support during the great mutiny. But the times were different after the First World War, Muslims of the Punjab had begun going communist knowing the insignificance of the conversion issues. Sikhs were become ardent votaries of total independence for India and had kept the *Ghadar* movement alive that had its beginnings among the NRS of California. The patriotic Indians now desired attention to economic issues and wanted effort of all Indians for freedom, democracy and development. The rise and martyrdom of Bhagat Singh and enthusiastic following of Netaji, vociferous success of Mahatma Gandhi's liberation movement and slogans of "Do or Die" were common currency. After half a century of freedom and head counting democracy, the conversion problem is only bothering the Christian missionary societies whose financial support from the gullible public in the west is on the basis of conversions affected by them. Within India the service role of the Christian missions still extracts willing respect. The emphasis is now on the modernization and development of the country for the entire people.

5.5 Bridges of Understanding

The coastal trade between India and Iran had passed into the hands of Arabs. The Muslim merchants were welcome in Indian coastal towns. The early opposition to Islam was from the Arab idol worshippers. The Hindu idol worship was best explained by Akbar who agreed that an idol was not god but it only was an imagined symbol for the attention of the worshipper. The living together in villages brought home to both Hindus and Muslims the natural ethical behaviour of all. For centuries Asokan edicts have been propagating ethical behaviour throughout Asia. Hindu Philosophy and Islamic ethics converged on the humanist behaviour. As a self-induced policy, Arya Samaj very much active in the Punjab and Sikhism refrained from idol worship. Muslims also reminded themselves that God had been illuminating other peoples at other times. Muslims believed that the Koran was the perfect revelation from God and there could be no prophet to succeed Mohammed. The Hindus did not limit God in this way and would consider on merits any further progress in religion and spirituality but they believed in everyone's right to accept or not any new ideas in the way scientists treat new explanations and new discoveries and inventions. Muslims have been disowning their thinkers when they stepped out of line, but the Punjabees loved their Sufi saints and the romantic poems about mundane and spiritual love or the poetry of Amir Khusro and Raskhan, Guru Nanak and Baba Dayal were universal favourites. Hindu and Muslim fanaticism is of recent vintage and will vanish together through further experience of these religions as these must blossom in freedom and peace and in the environment of science and technology.

5.6 Jats of the Punjab

There are Hindu Jats and Muslim Jats as well as Sikh Jats. Punjabees are easily classified as Jats and non-Jats. Jats are distinct from natives occupying Punjab from Vedic times. When Buddhism travelled into Central Asia, the way was shown to many tribes to come to the holy land of the Hindu-Buddhists. First to travel along the Himalayan trail were the Jats of Tashkent and Bukhara region. Later much larger numbers came from the original home of the Jats in west Asia near the Caspian Sea. These Jats trailed behind the Sans and Kushans. While the Sans and Kushans came waging war and established petty Hindu-Buddhist kingdoms in central India like the ones established by the Greeks, the Jats settled near Sialkot or southwards to the south-west of Delhi. The Hindu-Buddhist kingdoms and empire lasted only couple of centuries, but the Jats in their rough and tough wisdom lasted as tough and hard working rural Punjabees till today. They have their own caste panchayats and guide the successive generations in the Punjab in the culture of tolerance and the Jat way about how to live a happy and busy life. The life of the Jats and Ahirs revolves around agriculture and animal husbandry respectively. There are innumerable sayings about Jat humor primarily of wisdom in innocuous ways. The apparent simplicity only camouflages full understanding. A Jat can belong to any religion but will never be a fanatic. The Jats seem to be extra Jat-like when they are also Sikhs. When they did not provide leaders to a Sikh Misl, the Sikh Misls saw to it that the Jats were not disturbed. Jats would have ruled all Punjabees but for the Muslim Punjabees plumping for partition of the Punjab. Before partition, the Jats were running the government in the Punjab through Sir Sikandar Hayat Khan. Muslim Zamidars mostly were also Jats. The Hindu Jats dominate Haryana and the Sikh Jats the Punjab. Jats join Indian armed forces in large numbers. Jats created a strong Jat state under the leadership of Suraj Mal of Deeg near Mathura after continuous despoiling of Mughal convoys and camps usually of both the contending factions for the imperial crown of Delhi. The Jats of the imperial district from Delhi to Agra were the best gainers from the turmoil in Mughal domain primarily from atrocities at Mathura and long absence in fruitless warfare of the Mughal emperor in the Deccan for thirty years. The Jat quality for easy comradery and guaranteed reprisal for loss is illustrated throughout the rise of the Jats. The area south-west of Delhi devastated by the marches of various victorious or avenging armies particularly after the capture of Delhi by the British from the mutineers, was depopulated and the entire region became overgrown with jungle and bush. It was quietly occupied and rejuvenated by the Jats and it is now developing at a fast rate. The Punjabees now contain a large number of Jats and Balochies. They luckily have kept aloof from each other's holdings. Sikhs are respected by both for their matching tenacity and many Sikhs are also Jats who provide leadership to the Phulkian Sikh states. It is conceded that the panchayati village democracy so dear to Punjabees was first introduced centuries ago by the Jat immigrants. Raja Rasalu, the folk hero of the Punjab was a Jat.

5.7 Baptism through Suffering and Sacrifice in a just Cause

Punjabees have shown their ability to suffer by passing through the inglorious conquest of the Sultans from across the Indus and then forbearance and adaptability by living for centuries as pawns or mercenaries of non-mulki kings. They have shown their valour in the imperial armies including those of the Mughals or the British when they swept over Asia and Africa. In order to become free in a free and democratic India they had to demonstrate highest reaches of sacrifice and sustained effort. This they did when they died unarmed from the British bullets at Jallianwala Bagh of Amritsar or wrenched the control of their Gurdwaras (Sikh temples) from the usurper *mahants* . They were second to none in the civil disobedience and boycott movements begun by Gandhian leadership of the country. They carried their share of the violent revolutionary movement under the leadership of the Babas of *gadr* fame, of Bhagat Singh or of Netaji. In 1942, Punjab Congress-men did their share of confrontation with the colonial authorities with Rajendra of Batala as the appointed Congress leader. Most Punjab Congress-men were in jail from 1942 to 1946. Lately in free India Punjabees bore the brunt with others of the Pakistan's aggressive wars or of terrorism in Kashmir or aggressive infiltration in Kargil.

5.8 Punjab Villages

The Punjab villages had been self-governing from ancient times. When Ghauri's deputy ruled at Delhi in place of a Rajput king, it did not matter much; there being many intermediaries between the villager and the king. The village continued to pay the same taxes collected by the local *patwari* or the *raja* who then took care of the share of the king. Out of the rest of the produce, the local temple continued to have its share for the upkeep of the temple and the local Brahman who helped in religious observances of the people. Later the village will also support a *maulvi* if few families converted to Islam. The conversions were rare and usually happened only if too much temptation like freedom from severe punishment for a crime came one's way or some one became personally obliged to the Kazi or the governor. For the sake of spiritual solace or religious conviction, it was not customary to convert. Hindus could always embrace with open mind any new teaching or preaching if it appealed to them. That was how most of them became Hindu-Buddhist but shed the Buddhist Sangha when the discipline of the Sangha declined and the peaceful approach of the Buddhists lost the political power in the Punjab first to Sakas and then to Huns and Kushans, and the country retrieved its freedom only by the efforts of Shaivite Hindus and Rajputs or warlike Aggarwals and Aroras serving Jains and Hindu traders. The foreigners: Sakas, Huns and Kushans came as Buddhists but those who remained like the Greeks and Afghans before them merged as Jats and Hindus with the local population. The discriminatory Jaziya tax on non-Muslims was imposed later and sometimes cancelled. The situation remained like this even when slowly the majority of Punjabees in Punjab (P) became Muslim before the time of Maharaja Ranjit Singh. The Muslim kings of Punjab stationed at Delhi had treaty relations with the Hindu rulers of Taxila, Srinagar, Jammu, Kangra and Sialkot in order to protect their northern flank when they had set their greedy eyes on various rich temple towns to the East and South of Delhi. The Islamic rulers did not interfere with the pilgrim traffic to Kurukshetra and helped to maintain its sanctity and also pilgrims brought in trade and more taxes. Those who have seen the co-existence modė of life in the Hindu and Muslim princely states of the Punjab before partition like Kapurthala and Malerkotla, can understand the coexistence in the early Islamic Punjab.

The Greek-Persian remnants around Lahore attacked and destroyed Sanghol in the sixth century A.D. and history books call it the massacre of the Buddhists in the Punjab by the Hindus of the Punjab! Conversely, the Hindus led by rulers of Sialkot defeated the Greek- Persian Mehergul and restored Punjab to cultural three strips, one in the north under the influence of Hindu-Buddhists of Taxila in the west and Hindu republics of Bilaspur-Adi Badri in the east. The central strip around the communication route between Delhi and Attock which also would contain the track of the Grand Trunk (G.T.) Road built by Afghan power at Delhi. The third strip extended from Delhi through Rohtak, Hissar and Bathinda to Multan and then across the Indus river to terminate in Bannu-Kohat region, later popularly called the Mughal route as distinct from Sher Shah's GT road. More trade went along the Mughal route supported by the traders of the third strip both in India and in Gazni. It was the control of this trade that set Prithviraj of Delhi-Ajmer against the Ghauri kings of Gazni. Most of the plains of the Punjab were ruled up to the defeat of Prithviraj by occupants of scattered forts by adventurers from the refugees from the Shahi territories in the west of the Indus river after their unsuccessful struggle with the Arab-Iranian forces for two centuries. It was during this period between the fall of Sanghol and Mehergul to the fall of Delhi that the Punjabees in the three strips of the Punjab almost shaped modern Hinduism before its recorded happening through the well documented efforts of Shankaracharya in the eighth century A.D. The foundation was of Harrapan Pashupati and Kuru-desh pre-Buddhist Vedic-Hindu ethics. As stated earlier, their religion was essentially co-existence and humanism.

Centuries of civilized life in the Punjab villages did not disappear with the defeat of Prithvi Raj at Traori near Delhi.

If some one converted to Islam in a village, he having been assured of pardon by an Islamic court or as a result of being a follower of a Muslim man at arms getting as a bounty the powers over a Punjabee village. The Muslims in the village were not treated as out-castes but carried on their normal participation in the social affairs of the village. The Muslim was considered to have chosen an inferior religion leaving the freedom of belief exercised by the Hindus within the fold. The minority took more than a thousand years to rebel against the Hindus for the constraints in day-to-day life. The lowly castes and depressed classes never rebelled, the controls and brain washing of all was so severe.

5.9 Hindus of the Punjab

Hindus of the Punjab are the chastised remnants of ancient Punjabees. Their ancestors preferred to stay alive under Muslim domination sticking to their cocoons of caste and sub-caste. Brahmans continued in their jobs of being the wise-heads for the villagers and kept up their convictions and contentions in philosophical discussions. The Kshatriyas either were killed or sought army jobs with other masters all welcoming a new recruit. Traders and bankers flourished and were the last resort for borrowing by the Muslim gentry and Muslim peasants, always short of cash. At least one family of Hindu money lender survived in each village from India to Turkestan up to the World War of the twentieth century. Since the message from the *Gita* was loud and clear that God himself takes a hand in the life of the people when there is evidence of damage to the faithful almost beyond repair. The Punjabees had boldly settled down to finding solace in joint myths of the Hindus and Muslims. They sang about Guga pir who was dear to both and of Puran Bhagat, and Raja Rasalu who was the last Punjab hero. He was the elder brother of Puran Bhagat and personally killed in single combat the Muslim king of Attock when he interfered with peaceful travel of citizens across the Indus. Many a Muslim Shah and pious Muslims from far away sought to make India their home for the basic god fearing nature of the Punjabees. Suddenly invasions of the dispossessed Mughals from across the borders with new found zeal for setting up a Mughal kingdom in India had started. They gathered large invading army keen on loot in the Punjab. Hindus were now expecting the miracle of having God incarnate among them according to the promise in their scriptures. They hailed Guru Nanak as the promised Rama incarnate, when Guru Nanak inspired universal respect for his bold statements of truth about God and soul and their intimate relationship to be burnished bright by reciting God's name. Hindus brought up at least one child of the family as a Guru's disciple known as Sikh. Soon a new Sikh mythology developed that Guru Nanak was a prophet in the mould of Prophet Mohammed with directly perceived knowledge of God and being blessed with all wisdom. The Sikhs had the belief that there was continuation of Guru Nanak's spark in the following Gurus up to Guru Govind Singh who terminated the line of Sikh Gurus and declared their words enshrined among other sayings of some Hindu and Muslim saints in the Guru Granth Sahib as their Guru for all times. Guru Govind Singh also gave a new look, a military face to the Sikhs and raised the Khalsa, an army of Sikhs. The anarchy and mis-government of Delhi emperor's minions was so desperately bad that the Khalsa was always mobilized for attack or defence. The Hindu admirers of the Gurus thought that mobilization should be only for the youth they had dedicated to the Guru and the others could be known as sympathizers to be known as Sahajdhari Sikhs. This would have worked well but for the long range aims of the British overlords after the defeat of the Khalsa at the hands of the British Indian army primarily because of ineptness of the Khalsa leadership after Maharaja Ranjit Singh. Its leadership was infiltrated by ambitious men at the top who were willing to help British win for a price. The British divided the Punjabees by colonial democracy with communal award for voting. Now the Sikhs wanted only the Sikhs displaying the prescribed five "Ks" as entitled to vote as Sikhs and practically debarred Hindus to vote with the Sikhs. As a reaction to this, Hindu communalists also woke up to find all kinds of differences with the Sikhs and many Hindus named Hindi as their mother tongue just because the Sikhs declared for Punjabi language written in Gurumukhi script. The Punjabees now got restricted to few Muslim minority districts of the Punjab out of which present Punjab(I) is constituted. For our purpose Punjabees are the people living in Punjab(I), Punjab (P), Haryana, Delhi, Agra, Meerut and Himachal and some more other adjoining areas. The Punjabi Hindus are the true secularists finding it ridiculous to convert from one religion to another. All religions originate in truth and new insights when available are automatically gifts for any one who is ready to imbibe them and wait even for still better ones. Religion can also develop like science with experience and more understanding and further application of better observations and further flights of reason. Even in the days of Aurangzeb, often named as violently spreading Islam in India, Hinduism flourished all over India and merged in the east and west with popular Islam. The Punjab was a mixing bowl of Zoroastrian and Greek as well as Central Asian tribal lore with beliefs that had been developing in India starting with humanism and secularism.

5.10 Punjab after Expulsion of Huns

The Punjab became stable in the three strips mentioned above. Heun Tsang's visit to Sanghol is illustrative of the importance of Buddhism in the affairs of the Punjab. The Punjabees were already becoming more and more Hindu-Buddhists with temples also containing Shivlings and Naga *devatas* and occasional *devi* idols adored by both Hindus and Buddhists now succumbing to slow spread of syncretic beliefs involving magic and *Tantra*. The middle strip Punjabees were still having remnants of fire worship escalated to Sun worship mixed with hankering for a caring

God as expressed in the concepts of Bodhisattvas and incarnations of Vishnu with devotion to sacred sites of Kurukshetra and reverence for sacred rivers. The Punjabees in the south were under the influence of Jains and non-violent living, i.e. by trade and commerce. The Punjab trade across Kashmir continued to grow with the influence of Kashmir rulers and their connection with the Hindu and Buddhist rulers of Afghan kingdoms bordering the Indus. The Hindu, the Buddhist and the Jain asceticism had created a new section of roaming *sadhus*, *vairagis*, musicians and entertainers who enriched the Punjab village life in various ways. Every village boasted of wrestling and acrobatic practice and Yogis started having their centres all over the countryside and soon would convert to Muslim Takyas around the grave of a local *sadhu* or *faqir*. The worship of graves was the popular interpretation of worship of stupas and relics and living Jain saints or dead *sati's*. The ancient Punjabee warriors flocked to the new Khatri profession of banking and retail trade. The *yogis* claimed to be disciples of Gorakhnath with headquarters near Jhelum became popular custodians of Hindu humanism and stayed as its mouth piece for centuries, one Gorakhnath leading to the next guru Gorakhnath up to times of Aurangzeb. In Punjabi folk literature, he is the voice of common sense and credited with magical powers.

5.11 Muslim Punjabees

After the fall back towards the Indus of the Hindu Shahi kings of Kabul, the Muslim peaceful penetration occurred into ancient Iranian-Greek occupied zone of the Punjab broadly extending from the stretches of Indus to Lahore in the centre of Punjab. There was a population having a majority of Hindus and steadily growing number of Muslims in this zone. This is the area where Muslims coexisted with the Hindus at first in majority but later in minority. The zone was prosperous because of productive irrigated land and extensive pastures for goats and horses. The people together with those of Taxila and Kangra participated with donkey loads of merchandise in the rich Punjab-Turkestan trade.

5.12 Neo-Muslim

The Punjabi Muslims were mostly natives of the Punjab during the early Delhi Sultanate period. The conquering Muslim armies did not bring many colonizing Muslims. Even the Muslim soldiers from across the Indus were neo-Muslims. Later, towards the end of the rule of Delhi Sultans and before Mughal rule was firmly established, there was considerable immigration of Baloch people from land hunger, who came armed but could find haven in the uninhabited area of south western Punjab without much difficulty. Same thing happened at the end of the rule of Ranjit Singh and there was fierce conflict of Baloch immigrants or those already settled in villages within reach of the Sikh Misls. On the whole the Baloch immigrants increased the Muslim population of west Punjab. The native converts kept moving east where they were more prosperous in the fertile lands. The Muslims included Sunnis and Shias and the newly started sect of Ahmediyas as well as Ahl-i-Hadith. (The Shias and Sunnis used separate mosques.) The Muslim jagirdars also attracted them to new jagirs in Jammu, Himachal, and northern forested areas of Haryana and U.P. They peacefully penetrated into Hindu villages under the protection of Sufi saints and Sufi Takias already established, e.g. in Bahraich. The Muslim Takias in these parts are flourishing in peace and have religious links with Arab rulers of the middle east. There was a continuous string of Muslim Takias, well endowed tombs and khankas from Multan to Bahraich in U.P. and beyond. Many local Hindus also revered the saintly heads of takias as gurus in day-to-day life. The Muslim rulers at Delhi preferred the prominent Sufis to proceed on towards Bengal where the need of spreading Islam seemed to be greater. The eastern part of India was dubbed by them as a hell bereft of Islam but loaded with food. Prominent Sufis near Delhi were unpopular with the government since they befriended the Hindus and obstructed the rampant exploitation of the Hindu subjects. The villagers were tolerant and non-violent, preferred segregated living areas, were keen on ritual and *bhakti*. Hindus had traditional goals of *kam, arth,* and *moksha*.

5.13 The Sufis

The Sufis were a Muslim sect who had stuck to ancient worship of God through love expressed in song and dance. They worshipped relics and tombs, surely a remnant of Asian dallience with Buddhism, spread far and wide from Kashmir to Peshawar. The Sufis had been expelled almost from Egypt and Iran, but were settling peacefully as well as bringing new converts to their kind of Islam. A branch of Sufis would be the Rishis of Kashmir who spread Islam there. The Hindus in Punjab villages were happy to have Sufis and Sufi saintly persons known there as " Shah Ji". An interesting occurrence comes to my mind, a delegation of Ulema and intellectuals from Pakistan came in peace to persuade the Kashmiris to plump for Pakistan and enjoy freedom in an Islamic State there. A Kashmiri Muslim in the audience hackled him by saying that they were not like ordinary Muslims in Pakistan given to hatred of non-Muslims, but were Muslims converted by Kashmiri Rishis to Islam, which was possibly an alternative way to reach God's love for humanity. The Sufis were convinced that a human guide was necessary for the spiritual path to God realization. Sufi pirs initiated many bright young men in their respective Silsilas or factions. A young man need not belong to a single Silsila. A uniform requirement was a life deliberately chosen of poverty or practically that of an ascetic. The Sufis tried to be loyal Shias or Sunni Mussalmans but were prone to lead a life of a rebel in a conformist world. Finding the life in India among Hindus more congenial, they were popular in Hindu villages too. It was from a Sufi Shah ji, that I first learnt good treatment of dumb animals and not to hurt any living being, a bird or a dog. Sufis came in hordes into India. All the caravan routes were dotted with Sufi stations to help the travellers. Sufis did not suspect all music and dance. They held singing session after the mid-day meal often attended by Hindus and Muslims alike.

In India the most famous Sufi saint was Nizam-ud-din Auliya and his Chishtiya Silsila disciples set up many takiyas (centres) far and wide. This Silsila was well established in East Bengal. Amir Khusro a high up lord in the court of the Sultan at Delhi became a disciple of the Auliya. He was a Poet of Hindi, language of the people. He sung songs of love of God of the Sufis and preferred to spend most of his time with the Auliya even neglecting to appear in the king's court. He had sympathy for the suffering subjects. The Sufis asserted their independence of Sunni dominated officialdom and often forfeited their independence at Delhi. Bengal was considered to be a rebel state and a strong hold of Sufi Silsilas. Many Sufis were encouraged or driven to go to Bengal. There they were useful to the Sultan in spreading Islam or fighting for expansion of Islamic rule. The hold of Sunnis and Delhi Kazis was not so strong there. The local Muslims congregated in mosques for Friday prayers, but their chief meeting place were the Sufi khanqas usually next to tombs of Sufi saints. Sufis permitted dance and music and drinking declared taboo by the Sunnis. They were first to join battle and usually refused recognition for the military feats. They started community *langars* as later done by Sikhs in the Punjab. There was fraternal relationships of the Sikh gurus with the Sufi pirs. The Muslims honoured Guru Nanak as a Sufi Pir.

The Sufis of Bengal under the influence of Bengal Vaishnavism advised their flock that charity should not differentiate between Hindus and Muslims. Around that period, Hindus and Buddhists invented *Tantra* to miraculously force gods to help mankind and individual initiates. Tantra was enemy of solid effort by natural means and ultimately succumbed to the practical nature of Muslim and Sufi doctrines buttressed by belief in the kindness and love of God for mankind. All over north India the cult of Gorakhnath and his disciples based on Yoga, meditation, service and magic had spread. Nath Yogis often appear to sympathize with the suffering characters in Sufi romances, e.g. in Heer Ranjha of the Punjab. The common people of Bengal came together in the nineteenth century to produce a composite Hindu-Muslim or Indian culture. Bengal was the chief Sufi centre in the Islamic world. The Ilya Shahi dynasty of Bengal provided a stimulus to the growth of composite Bengali culture. But the Hindu-Muslim unity turned into two nation divide between the two World Wars by the machinations of the British manipulation of voting rights. The flexibility of the Sufis is in sharp contrast to the inflexibility of the orthodox. The goal of Hindu and Sufi mysticism is the same and the methodology to achieve it is also the same. Rumi had expressed Sufi love of God in Persian poetry.

Baba Farid was the most famous Sufi of the Punjab. Data Gunj Bakhsh with his mausoleum in the outskirts of Lahore had many Hindu and Muslim devotees seeking his favours. He had dozens of khadims attending at the mausoleum looking to the comfort and facilities for praying for the Data's favours. Nizam-ud-din Auliya was a disciple of Baba Farid. Baba Farid exalted austerity and meditation. In eastern U.P. the Sharqui dynasty of Jaunpur helped the establishment of many Silsilas. The fusion of Sufi and Nath philosophy was personified in Shah Madar, the accepted mythical head of all semi-religious entertainers. Lal Ded, the famous Hindu convert to Islam and a poet in her own right started the Rishi Silsila in Kashmir to which many Kashmiri Muslims belong.

Mystic conception of Reality is the same of Sufis and Sahaj Shaivites which lay the prevailing faith of Hindus in the olden days. A final step in the ladder to supreme bliss was the recognition of a suitable guru or teacher (*marg-darshak* in Sanskrit). This is also the widespread belief of the Hindus which spelled the fast growth of Sikhism in the Punjab. A large number of Nath yogis popularized syncretism or current Indian culture. To yogis, prophet Mohammed was a disciple of a yogi of Gujarat ! The Sufis found nothing different in the profession of faith in Love of God by the Vaishnavites. The popularity of Vaishnava items in Sufi rituals was a new development in the Indian theme of unity in diversity. Guru Nanak diverged from the yogic and Sufi thought and regarded asceticism as a useless burden for a life of purity and righteousness.

Baba Farid was the most famous Sufi of the Punjab. Data Ganj Bakhsh wit his impressive mausoleum near Santnagar of Lahore had many Hindu and Muslim devotees. Nizam-ud-Din Auliya of Delhi was one his disciples. Baba Farid exalted austerity and meditation like many devout Punjabees.

The mixed population was intrinsically secular and bound with villager's tradition which was so well depicted in the poems of Waris Shah and other Sufi poets.

From about 1500 A.D. to the departure of the British rulers of Punjab in 1947, the Muslims constituted the majority of Punjabees.

6 THE SIKHS

6.1 Introduction

Guru Nanak (1469-1539) was the fulfilment of the promise made in the *Gita* that God is sure to reincarnate Himself among mankind when there is chaos in the world due to weakening of the sense of Dharma or duty in the people. The Punjabees were thoroughly beaten into submission and the sultan ruled at Delhi. The Muslim Kazis and jagirdars appointed through their military service ruled the entire land. The age-old caste system held, allowing new Muslims and victorious strangers to find their niche in the prevalent caste system. Often they were treated as a separate caste. The citizens had two broad divisions, Muslim and non-Muslim. The Kazi ruled according to the Islamic laws. Punishments could be waived if the culprit was prepared to convert to Islam. Hindus were exploited through special taxes and other demands like extra labour for the upper strata of society. No new Hindu temples could be built and any gold or silver or even metallic vessels would be taken away under some excuse or the other. Barring the general desecration of temples and the abduction of Hindu women at the initial occupation of Hindu lands, there was discipline and the rulers gave a modicum of liberty and safety to the Hindus to keep on patiently and diligently working and producing wealth for the benefit of the upper castes and the state. The enterprising Hindus converged on the professions of banking, shop keeping and trade and made success. Most of the "well-to-do" Muslim gentry including new royalty became debtors to

Hindu money lenders. The Hindus became more concerned with rituals and caste observances believing that their laxity was the cause of neglect by their gods. The caste system became harsher and lower castes and artisans were ground down by the legitimate as well as unlawful demands of the upper classes and the government machinery. The creativity in religion suffered both from internal opposition as well as challenge from Islamic opposition backed by the rules framed for the spread of Muslim supremacy. A digression is necessary to bring up-to-date the ferment that spread in the middle east by the revelation of the Koran in Arabia and its spread to Asia and Africa.

6.2 Rise of Delhi Sultanate

Mohammed, the messenger of God brought the Koranic verses directly inspired by the true God. He met violent opposition from the entrenched followers of the ancient Arab faith in superstitions about planets, omens and gods of ancient times and tribes. He overcame all opposition and created his Muslim following which he imbued with military discipline and indomitable courage out to spread the new monotheistic faith in the whole world. Islam spread fast following victories in the battle field over Iran and Iraq, the two ancient imperial powers of West Asia. Iranian empire under the victorious Macedonian Alexander had been extended from the shores of the Caspian to the Indus across Afghanistan and the Punjab. The Arab -Iranean power under the Muslim Caliph of Baghdad felt proprietary right to rule over the old imperial territories, but they could not prevail over the Shahi kingdoms in Afghanistan-Punjab. Their relentless pressure of repeated invasions for two centuries was successful in storming Kabul towards the close of the tenth century. The Caliph had earlier in the eighth century vanquished all opposition in their invasion of the Sind province of India and had their governor at Sukkur. Any further incursions northwards were rebuffed by the Rajput king of Mewar and the condition of imposed peace on the Caliph was that Islamic forces will not commit any further inroads into India from Sind. The Arabs abided by the treaty provisions. Later expansion into India was from Batoch move northwards to Multan and Muslim armies from Afghanistan towards Lahore. The Punjabees organized spirited counter-attacks under the leadership of rulers of Kangra and Bathinda and pressed forward to Peshawer where they suffered a disastrous defeat partly by inadequacy of command in a loosely organized confederate army and partly by misfortune. The armies of Mohammed Ghauri defeated various kings of Punjab and of the Indian territories around Delhi. They occupied Delhi in early thirteenth century when the Delhi Sultanate was established with the set purpose of spreading Islam. Hindus had concentrated their wealth in temples where idol worship was regularly carried out. Islam was particularly against idol worship or bringing up any god or man to the level of the one God they worshipped. The Islamic faith combined with iconoclastic zeal fulfilled also the wildest dreams of loot of the Muslim tribesmen. The Islamic armies had no dearth of enthusiastic recruits. India's power was distributed in petty kingdoms and free self-contained villages. In the absence of a clear vision of India as a threatened nation, they could never pull a planned united stand against the invaders right up to the complete loss of freedom of the whole country first to the Mughals and later to the British colonial armies. They were to win many combats but lost wars and territories piece by piece. The only Indian power that would rise to contend for supremacy was the secular power that arose in the Punjab pursuing the righteous path of love and justice shown by Guru Nanak. It was the secular state centred at Lahore of Maharaja Ranjit Singh. The Khalsa armies of Punjab could not find the same kind of dedicated patriotic leadership as provided by Maharaja Ranjit Singh in his lifetime. The lesson of History was that Indian freedom and military strength pivoted on secularism and willingness to stay abreast of other states in the arts of peace and sciences of warfare. The country must build up its required leadership and strength in peace and be alert to weed out continuously the weak links or to provide further training where necessary.

Anyone not fully committed to secularism as explained by Nehru or in the Constitution of India is potentially a weak link.

6.3 Mughals on the Horizon

Mughals occupied a small territory in China in competition with Mongols, Tibetans, Kushans and Huns. Following the Hun tradition, a band of Mughals ventured south to win a state of their own. Perceiving the threat, the Sultans of Delhi strengthened the border defences in the north. The Mughals attacked Lahore in 1240 A.D., but the Afghan governor repulsed the attack with the help of the Hindu king of Kashmir, but the Mughals were not disheartened and kept continuous probing raids on the Indian empire.

Lodhi emperor of Delhi was embroiled in rebellions of his governors in the early sixteenth century. He could count only on his able minister, Hemu, a Hindu officer who had managed each time to overcome various rebellions occurring in quick succession. The courtiers were aware that Hemu was all powerful in the empire and were secretly in intrigue with the Mughals for their own advancement if the emperor and his *confidante* Hemu could be ousted by the Mughals who were after all their co-religionists. As a consequence, Baber with a compact force of 10,000 horsemen came to offer combat to the Lodhi emperor at Panipat, the famous battle ground where fate of many Delhi rulers was decided. The Lodhi king was defeated and Baber entered Delhi as conqueror on 22nd April 1526. (In the same way would Clive enter Murshidabad after the so called battle of Plassey in 1757 A.D.). Baber drove out the Afghan garrisons from Lahore and Saharanpur to seek shelter at Rohilkhand or Alwar. Baber died at Agra in 1526. The Afghan general Sher Shah, the governor of Eastern Territories retired to his eastern capital and resolved to recover Delhi from Baber's successor Humayun, in which he succeeded in 1540. Sher Shah died in 1545. Humayun escaped to Iran. He came back with a fully equipped contingent and sufficient resources granted by the Iran's Shia emperor, with which he wrested Delhi from Suri's weak successors. Humayun again became the king at Delhi. Humayun died in a palace accident. On hearing this at Kalanaur about 200 km away from Delhi, Humayun's general Bairam Khan immediately crowned Humayun's son Akbar as the successor and proceeded towards Delhi. They had to defeat Hemu, the elected ruler of Delhi in the absence of any able Lodhi or Suri contender. In the second battle of Panipat in 1558, Hemu was defeated when he was killed in battle by a chance arrow in the way the king of the Saxons died at Hastings in England leading to the Norman occupation of England.

6.4 Nanak Recognized

When Baber advanced towards Panipat from Lahore, his soldiers would round up all able bodied men on the way for possible labour. In the prison camp at Saidpur the soldiers were surprised to find a corner of peace and the prisoners singing praise of the lord around a holy man. The matter was reported to Baber. The holy man was Nanak who was a philosopher, poet, composer and a musician. Many Sufi saints and poets had entered India in the wake of Afghan success. Baber apparently revered such saintly people. He ordered the release of Nanak and all in the prison camp and ordered his soldiers to take care and not to cause hardship to any saintly person.

Nanak was already well known for his piety and questioning mind since his childhood. He was the son of a land official in Talwandi, a village near Lahore. Nanak would sing his own compositions and he would gather listeners as he wandered from village to village. He asked people to be truly pious and not go for show of worship. He railed against superstitions and empty gestures of both Hindus and Muslims. According to him, God can be reached through love of fellow men and one's resolve to be pure at heart. Such a resolution is strengthened by repeating His name and by *Satsang*, i.e. company of superior souls. He was the " Bhakta" incarnate of one formless God. Nanak's philosophy was simple and expressed in song in the popular language of the country which was Punjabi as understood practically all over India due to the still remembered instructions of the Buddha and Mahavira as well as Brahmanical myths when they talked of folk devotion to God or to their particular deity. Worship in temples had become complicated. It was beset with donations to the Brahmans and extortions through the exploitation of the gullible populace with talk of miracles, and mediation of the Brahmans or the Mullah, the Muslim knowing parrot-wise his Koran. The followers of the Guru were called Sikhs—Punjabi for disciples; there were no priests or intermediaries between a person and a most kind God. A religious Sikh up to the partition of India was a humanist like the Hindu and aware of Hindu mythology and Buddhist creed as well as the Jain insistence on non-violence. The Sikhs had ready communication with the Sufis and other devotees of God. The Hindus soon began to regard guru Nanak as an incarnation of Lord Rama and some regarded Guru Nanak as their Guru and venerated him almost like God Himself. The Sikhs believe in 10 Gurus one after the other from Guru Nanak. The last or the 10th Guru, Guru Gobind Singh declared that there would be no more human Gurus and for all time people were to regard Guru Granth Sahib, the holy book of the Sikhs in which are inscribed the teachings in the form of musical statements of the Sikh religion covering all aspects. The Granth also includes chosen words of other

Hindu and Muslim saints and holy men. The songs of the humanist Kabir are particularly popular. Guru Nanak travelled far and wide in the Punjab, in India and abroad. He visited Tibet, most pilgrim centres of India and pilgrim centres of Islam in Arabia, Iraq and Turkey. All his travels were on foot across Iranian plateau, along the Caspian sea and across Afghanistan and all regions of India. His genius in poetic composition, setting the praise of God to music, giving answers to difficult religious enquiry in language of the people is the subject of ardent enquiry by learned people well-versed in western as well as Chinese and Indian philosophy and logic, in modern universities and institutes particularly of India and Pakistan. The first few gurus of the Sikhs laboured to compile the material for the scriptures which saw the light during the tenure of Guru Arjun, the fifth Guru who was also a martyr for his firmly held convictions and who refused to bend under torture at Lahore. He advised that the Sikhs though inclined to be peaceful, should be able to withstand injustice by standing up to the tyrant. The sixth guru, Guru Hargovind started moving with guards and wore full armour in public appearances. On account of adverse report by the governor at Sirhind, he was imprisoned in Gwalior fort. The Mughal emperor went to converse with him and he was so impressed that he released him with honour and showered distinctions on him. The ninth guru, Guru Teg Bahadur (1614-1675) became a martyr, being cruelly executed under the orders of the Mughal emperor who offered a pardon if he were to covert to Islam. The Guru had espoused the cause of the Hindus who were being debarred from wearing in Kashmir the sacred thread that was the symbol of being Hindus. The saga of the tenth guru is of courage in the face of continuous suffering. He was so much touched by the cruelty suffered by the public from the minions of the empire supposedly following the state policy of preferential treatment of only Muslims, that he wrote his famous Zafarnama in Persian poetry to emperor Aurangzeb summarizing it himself by stating that if the king does not attend to the sufferings of his subjects, the subjects have every right to rebel and depose him. As a result the local guardians of the Mughal empire subjected him to incessant warfare and cruelty. His family had to perish and his two small sons were bricked alive, a cruel Mughal punishment for those who refuse the offer of elevation if they abjure rebellious beliefs and become Muslim. The Guru was assassinated when he himself went south primarily for once again attempting to convert the emperor to peaceful ways, but the emperor had died already.

6.5 From Rebels to Rulers

Sikhism began as quintessence of Hinduism and in addition tried to accommodate Islam as much as possible in the common monotheism but through prevailing circumstances, it slowly became a creed of rebels who did their best to drive away the agents, Hindu or Muslim of the Mughal empire from the Punjab. Guru Nanak died in 1539 and Guru Govind Singh in 1707. Before his death the Guru had established the Khalsa, a brotherhood in arms of the Sikhs. St. Peter could at the crux of events deny his association with Christ, but the Guru made an effort by enjoining all Sikhs to wear their hair unshaven so that such denial could never arise. The Sikh gurus from Guru Nanak to Guru Govind Singh were the great Punjabees who awakened the public to throw off the yoke of Mughals and Pathans. They boldly preached and practiced a casteless society. Their lives were of traditional holy men who maintained that the righteous path has to be followed by ordinary worldly men and women. The Sikh gurus were reformers of the Hindu practices and railed against meaningless rituals, forced isolation of widows, and addiction to tobacco. The grateful public built gurdwaras at all sites that brought back the memory of a visit of the guru. The labours and sacrifices of the gurus are awe inspiring. The gurdwaras may be visited keeping Amritsar or Chandigarh as camping points. When Sikhs or the entire people of Punjab rebelled and Mughals requested their allies the Afghans to subdue them. About 150,000 Sikhs were murdered on sight since the empire paid for each such decapitation. The immediate leader of the Sikhs was Banda Bahadur Bairagi, a Rajput specially chosen and sent to the Punjab by the Guru to avenge the public for the Mughal atrocities. In a few years he had demolished all centres of Mughal or Afghan military presence. Eventually, the imperial resources prevailed and Banda was ensnared with almost a thousand of his trusted troops and all were paraded with halters around their necks and most cruelly put to death. The sacrifice could not be in vain. In spite of most stringent measures against the Sikhs, they were victorious. Having invented a new kind of guerrilla war of continuous warfare on the run and never giving the opposition a chance to tackle or overpower a sizeable body of insurgents. The dispersed leadership was extremely invisible. Every village contributed to the organization of a local *misl* or a fragment of rebel army. These fragments were to assist each other when necessary for any project started by any fragment. The Afghan governor of Sirhind, the infamous centre of Mughal power where two Sikh princes were bricked alive, tried to make peace with the Sikhs by inviting the Marathas to make it easy for him and the Sikhs to control Punjab then under severe attack from local agents of both Mughals and Afghans. The Marathas soon returned, but the Sikhs decimated both Mughal and Afghan agents. After the victory of the Afghan ruler at Panipat over the Marathas he returned to Kabul with nothing to show for his labours since all his gains, his loot and his baggage had been taken by the Sikhs expert in running raids. He had no option but to declare the Sikhs to be his heirs in the Punjab. His summation of the fighting quality of Sikhs was that he failed to deal with them in any manner. The Sikhs will not bargain for anything less than victory for themselves. Abdali fought the Marathas to smithereens but was helpless against a whole population of independent individual fighters. There was total destruction of Mughal or Afghan power in the Punjab. Punjab became the sole possession of Maharaja Ranjit Singh a leader of the Sikhs around Lahore. He won the submission of village after village of the Punjab from the independent Sikh Misls. The other imperial power in the country was the armed East India Company set-up by the British imperialism. There was devastation around Delhi because of the mutiny in the Company's Indian forces in 1857 and its suppression by the British in alliance with the Sikh rulers south of the Sutlej and passivity of the Punjab Sikh armies in the British occupied Punjab after the two Anglo-Sikh wars subsequent to the death of Maharaja Ranjit Singh about a decade earlier. The British officers managed to make an alliance with the rump of the Sikh leadership. They took care to disarm the company's Indian forces of occupation in the Punjab and over-awe the people by excessive terror and reprisals for any semblance of spirit. They helped extend irrigation in the Punjab and by liberally gifting land to the Sikhs and others allowed the Sikhs to spread all over the Punjab in relative prosperity. The idea of India being a nation is said to have been in the plans of the Mughals and the British. Indians themselves were devoted only to their petty kingdoms merrily existing on payment of fees and territory to the company. The British took over the Indian empire directly after 1857 and India started on the road to nationhood and later independence. Akbar and Maharaja Ranjit Singh had understood the value of a secular state and the idea was incorporated in the constitution of free India by Nehru.

Since Punjabees in their villages were total lords through their fighting Sikh Misls, there was a chance that they now start bickerings and lose their gains. Providence helped them by the appearance of Ranjit Singh, leader of the fighting group around Lahore. He by valour and tact won the Punjab villages one by one and welded them into a Sikh empire of the Punjab with Lahore as capital. His generals out-fought and subdued the Afghans and Afghanistan ceded considerable territory to the Sikhs to strengthen Punjab defences by many forts established by the Sikh empire beyond the Indus. Such a prepared defence never existed before Maharaja Ranjit Singh. The History of Punjab now became practically the history of the Sikhs. Only later, the British came to rule over the Punjab. In order to hold on to India, they sowed the seeds of communal conflict all around, and India has yet to completely eradicate the resulting disunity. India has been well served by Mahatma Gandhi whose creed was non violence and whose aim was to win over all opposition. He was a champion of peace that India has been blessed with after Guru Nanak. As Ranjit Singh served to make the dream of the Sikh gurus succeed in the Punjab, Jawaharlal Nehru and Sardar Patel helped India to tide over the times of troubles created by the shadow of true democracy thrust on India by the departing British. Now the world is aiming to get together in peace and to develop being fully alive to the magic of secularism and co-existence. UN governance through cooperating nations and peoples of the world will effectively bring about the Khalsa rule in the world, of the pure at heart as well as propagate kinship of the entire human family. The international utopia that must arise will be based on freedom, human rights, equality and secularism with continuously rising living standards of all humanity.

6.6 Community Life of the Sikhs

The Sikh character is moulded by Sikh elders mainly through incessant chanting and singing of old and new myths of human victory over obstacles with the merciful guidance of the Guru and the pleasure of God. The Punjabi altruistic nature, their willing sacrifice of time and money for the needy and their willingness to take up cudgels against a bully is brought to a passion with the Sikhs. The Punjab village is run by self-governance from pre-Vedic times. All religions of the Punjab, Sikh or Hindu, Muslim or Christian are deep down secular, though they allow the respective preachers to rail against inter-caste or inter-religious marriages. Recently the Akal Takht, the elected highest body aiming to protect Sikh traditions and culture have advised the Sikh youth not to fall in love with a non-Sikh girl. For a long time Christian and Muslim *chowkidars* (hide-bound elders aiming to herd the flock) have advised the respective youth that when they insist on marrying outside the pail, the spouse will have to first convert to the true religion before marriage or at least undertake to allow the children of their union to be brought up in the true faith. All this is against the dictates of love or the secular approach. There are scores of historical marriages both inter-caste or inter-religious accepted by the society and the friends of the marrying couple. May be, in the future, it will be enjoined that all marriages should preferably be outside one's caste or religion for better evenness in the Indian society. Hindus have a rather lenient view though they also side with the "chowkidars" in the villages once a "mixed " marriage seems to have ridden into stormy weather. The Sikh history is full of selfless sacrifice of thousands of Sikhs for the sake of freedom to live their social or religious life. The sacrifices of great renown are remembered after every Sunday's Gurdwara session of prayer and preaching. The Sikh prayer is for the welfare of all and not just for the Sikhs. The humanism of old is kept alive.

The Muslims are expected to donate at least 2.5 per cent of their income for religious charity. The Sikhs raised the figure to 10 per cent of income. The Gurdwaras that collect the charity are rich and there is natural urge to control Gurdwara funds. The Akalis who waged a struggle in the nineteenth and twentieth century to free the Gurdwaras from private control or the control of the head attendant (*mahant*), have been the democratic party in majority in the Gurdwara Prabandhak Committee (the elected body managing the Sikh shrines). Most Gurdwaras in the country are either accountable to this committee or the separate committee for Delhi. It has been the Gurdwara funds created and managed by the NRI Sikhs in Canada and USA that financed the Khalistan movement sponsored in part by the ISI of Pakistan when Pakistan encouraged all kinds of fissiparous tendencies in India. The Sikhs in India as well as abroad had become victims of slogans raised just before the partition by the British and their henchmen in India in various communities of India that Hindus of India will exploit the minorities like the Muslims, the Sikhs etc. The Sikhs settled outside India thought a struggle for Khalistan in India on the lines of Jews' struggle for Israel in the middle east, if successful will give better international face to them. The terrorists group Babbar Khalsa set up in the subcontinent is still pursuing the chimera of Khalistan with practically no popular backing anywhere. Similar logic have landed the Punjabees into a relatively small and compact Punjabi Suba (now the Punjab-I). After the linguisic re-organizaton of India most non-Sikh Punjabees live in Pakistan's Punjab or in Haryana. The Punjab Hindus frightened by the communalist leaning of the Akali leadership and insistence on the definition of a Sikh to be strictly one with unshorn hair and not just a claim to be a disciple of the Gurus, had started claiming Hindi to be their mother tongue like the non-Sikhs of Haryana. Delhi has now a Punjabee majority, but Delhi belongs to the capital region state of India with no particular linguistic problem. Delhi citizens learn all languages : Punjabi, Hindi and English with great felicity besides other languages when spoken at home. Most Punjabees are ready for the new world where all nations will live at peace under the UN umbrella and world development will bye-pass petty conflicts of national borders, community, language and creed as bad dreams of ignorant past. The Guru's forecast that Khalsa will prevail, will come to pass. The new Khalsa will be the force at the command of world leadership through consultations in the U.N. The Sikhs will surely play an honourable part in it as they did in the two world wars as well as in the freedom movement and in the defence of free India.

A cardinal principal of Sikh community life is *langar*, i.e. community meal where all are welcome to sit down together when volunteers serve the food on separate platters which has been cooked by volunteers in the common kitchen. The *langar* destroys distinctions of high and low or rich and poor. The concept of *langar* is now taken over by many religious and social organizations. A similar major community principle is that of *Kar Seva* literally labour in service. Punjabees have from times immemorial been engaged in cooperative work for village agriculture and village activities. The Sikhs when they resolve on any construction work, they invite people to donate funds and where possible also labour. The voluntary *Kar Seva* has supported many community projects especially construction of gurdwaras, community irrigation and village infrastructure like guest houses for pilgrims and availability of drinking water to way-farers etc. *Kar Seva* has also spread to all regions and communities, particularly in rural India.

We have left out the part played by *manjis, masands,* and *mahants* in the evolution of Sikh management of Gurdwaras and of funds. The gurus dismissed the individual collectors of charity funds when the system had outlived its advantage. The Sikhs had to wage a major non-violent struggle to get rid of *Mahants* who treated gurdwaras as their hereditary property and brazenly went against *sangat's* expectations. The Akali struggle against the *mahants* is a golden page in the non-violent struggles in the world that were successful through sacrifice and own suffering. Mahatma Gandhi called this struggle as the first in the fight for India's freedom through non-violence. In this non-violent struggle 400 volunteers lost their lives and 40,000 suffered jail sentences shelled out by the colonial courts committed to safeguard private property rights in the Punjab, alleged to be resting with the *mahants*.

6.7 Sikh Stewardship

It was customary for Sikhs to donate atleast 10 per cent of their income for the community. The political groups of the Sikhs try to control the Gurdwaras where the funds are collected. The competitive communalism of such groups when there is no physical danger to the community leads to demonstration of fanaticism and ultimately to terrorism against the fancied enemy or the 'lagging' members of the community itself. The Bhindranwala terrorism was basically for the control of the Akali Dal that was master of the gurdwara funds but lukewarm according to Bhindranwala for the goal of an independent Sikh state where political rights will be only with the Sikhs. The Muslim League's bloody but victorious struggle for Pakistan was his correct policy. The Khalistan movement was propelled by considerable Gurdwara funds from overseas primarily from Canada and had the political support of imperialism and Pakistan since these had an unfinished agenda of breaking up of India. India has emerged stronger after facing the Khalistan threat. All peace loving people are beginning to realize that the Guru's vision of enemy less world ruled by Khalsa could be a hint for the inevitable utopia (christened *mustopia* by the author) of world governance through all co-operating nations under the umbrella of a democratic U.N.

Guru Arjun had enacted a system of 22 Manjis or preaching districts which rose to become 52 Birs or Sangats under Guru Ram Das. The chief collector or Masand of the sangat tended to become a sort of dictator from the control of sangat's funds. The tenth Guru, when he created the Khalsa, disbanded the Masands, the Birs and the Manjis. The funds started often to be mis-spent by the Mahants who sometimes owned a gurdwara or were exercising hereditary upkeep of the gurdwara having been so employed at start of that Gurdwara in the manner of Brahman *pujaris* of Hindu temples. The Mahants were dislodged by the Akalis during the British control of the Punjab, after prolonged agitation and sacrifices. The Akalis succeeded in having legislation vesting control of all Gurdwaras and associated funds by the Sikh community which would elect a management body. The Mahants had disgraced themselves when they offered victor's symbol to the tyrant that had ordered the Jallianwala Bagh massacre or when they refused to allow certain Sikhs of low caste to join the congregation at the Darbar Sahib. The British acting as the constituted authority protecting the property rights of citizens, regarded the claimed rights of the Mahants as valid.

A contingent of protesting non-violent Sikhs during the anti-Mahant agitation was confronted by hired ruffians engaged by a Mahant Narain Das of Nankana Sahib. There was months long sustained non-violent agitation at Guruka-Bagh which was claimed as private property by the Mahant. The sacrifices of the Sikhs brought about a change in the public posture of the authorities. According to Mahatma Gandhi, the Akali victory was the first step in India's freedom by peaceful means. In this non-violent struggle of the Akalis, at least 400 Sikh volunteers lost their lives and about 40,000 suffered jail sentences. The Sikhs thus went through with flying colours in both non-violent and violent struggles. So that every gurdwara, church and temple is an inviting place for all Indians. We hope that in future apart from universal right of all Indians of free secular India to enter and if so inclined, participate in the worship ritual, a separate meditation or silent prayer room would exist in the premises on the lines of the Japanese Shinto shrines. The ancient hatreds and grievances have to be shelved. Whole of the country belongs to all Indians whatever anyone's religion or caste.

7 PUNJABEES IN ASCENDANT

7.1 Introduction

The Punjabees had almost forgotten their true ancient religion under the repeated blows of fanatic followers of Islam excited by the licence to loot Hindu wealth garnered by centuries of peaceful labour and trade with far-flung people who regarded the Hindus as world teachers of civilized pursuits. Hindus had been leaders in producing necessities as well as luxury items for trade and human happiness. The true piety of communal life had given place to selfishness and greed. They practically started believing their dolls and deities as powerful gods looking after them and this belief was easily destroyed when the temples were broken into by violent invaders who could be stopped only by superior violence. Sporadic heroes did arise like the famous General Ratbil of Arab chronicles who defeated the Arab armies surging northwards to Kabul in the eighth century A.D. Ratbil stood guard at Kabul for many decades, but was captured and converted to Islam, but he again erupted as a victor and the Hindu Shahi dynasty survived at Kabul and later on the Indus up to the tenth century A.D. Another Hindu hero was the Rajput chief Bapa Rawal who stopped the advance of the Arabs northwards from Sind. Among the Punjabees, the rulers of Bathinda, Kangra and Sialkot fought the tribal assaults from the west to practically a standstill affair but for the unfortunate death of Anandpal in a bitter fight at Peshawar where victory was snatched from him by the misadventure of his elephant running amuck. There was no idea of an Indian nation to be defended then for all time from inroads from the west. Fighting and invasion was a game played by all Indian kinglets from the Vedic age. Enslavement was never before in the cards. Thus due to lack of a true insight into the new value system of the Islamic hordes that got together to attack and enslave the Hindus, they could barely be allowed to live to labour for the new Sultans. The hope dawned only with the rekindling of the Hindu Dharma by the genius of Guru Nanak who was a poet and philosopher preaching love and brotherhood representing the essence of Hindu Bhakti and piety in the footsteps of the Buddha and Mahavira who had kindled the soul of India earlier as great Hindus of their day. The Sikhs as the followers of the great Guru and his successors culminating in the stoic warrior hero Guru Gobind Singh gave telling blows to the tyrants of Delhi and Kabul. And the Punjabees began to hold their head high giving blow for blow and showering love on the real pious Muslims and the Sufis who were like brothers of their Gurus. From the fall of Sirhind, the den of cruelty embodied in the entombment of living child hero sons of Guru Gobind Singh, the Punjabees had no quarrel with their national destiny.

7.2 Demolition of Mughal and Afghan Rule

The fighting tenth guru, the king of kings was assassinated when he went south with the expressed purpose of meeting the Mughal emperor Aurangzeb, but the emperor had died before the meeting. The Punjabees could not but avenge the terror unleashed against them by the Mughal minions who had also invited the Afghans to prop the tottering Delhi empire. The Guru had appointed a valiant leader from Rajputana, the Banda Bahadur of history who now led the Khalsa from victory to victory till he was cornered and imprisoned by the combined Mughal and Afghan forces near Gurdaspur. He was killed along with his companions most cruelly. This became the last nail in the coffin of the Mughal empire over the Punjab and the start of the end of Afghan aggression. The Afghan king Abdali made a dozen armed attacks on the Punjabees and at the end had to rue his failure to make any impression on the Punjabees except on their own terms, viz. recognition of their Guru's sway in the Punjab where the Sikh rulers of tiny villages set up mints to cast gold coins in the name of the Guru. Abdali and his successors at Kabul had utter failure in their quest of a Punjab empire as it had existed for few centuries in cohorts with the Mughals. The Mughal empire had lasted for that long on account of the secular policies pursued by Akbar and his insistence on selecting his military and civil associates in authority strictly on merit. He had abolished the discriminatory taxes on non-Muslim subjects and merchants. The Punjab had also prospered and the Akbar's beneficiaries included a very large number of non-Muslims both in the army as well as in civil governance. Only the pursuit of a fundamentalist Muslim empire at Delhi and intolerance of popular piety of the Punjabees as well as the disloyal treatment of the Marathas upset the Mughal apple cart that could not be again set up even with the exploits of aggressive Afghans who had earlier despoiled India of all her treasure by brazen aggression on Indian cities. The Afghan governor, Samad Khan started a reign of terror from Lahore. He also made a deal with Khalsa of Amritsar not to support Banda being encircled at Gurdaspur and in return agreed to allow Hindus to practice their religion with dignity from then on.

There was first a decentralized rule of the Sikh Misls all over the Punjab and later it got centralized through Maharaja Ranjit Singh, the democratically elected ruler of Lahore. Ranjit Singh, through his genius and fair dealings like those of Akbar, conquered and united under his personal rule whole of Punjab and adjoining areas of an empire created by his Dogra generals in Kashmir, Gilgit, Ladakh, and Chamba. His generals by spirited warfare and sense of fulfilling ancient eminence of the Punjab scattered all opposition in the southern and western Punjab. They built and occupied forts on both sides of the Indus to protect the Punjab domain in future. The Baloch power intruding into the Punjab north of Sukkur and in the western hills beyond the Indus was crushed but many Baloch Muslims were allowed to settle in peace in the western Punjab where they became sharers of Punjab prosperity. They now constitute the Muslim subjects of Pakistan Punjab.

The governors and rulers in the Punjab had continued the Mughal style of feudal rule including the grant of jagirs and creating petty rajas all over the country and having the fond hope that they will all understand their feudal loyalties and duties. Such fond hope was never fulfilled in all despotic rule including that of the maharaja even when it had some religious under pinning being regarded by many as Sikh rule when it was only the despotic rule of a secularist Sikh as expected of any pious Hindu or Sikh. When the Guru desired Punjabees to be neither Hindus nor Muslims, he really wanted them to be both that is not to quarrel among themselves. The Guru was respected by the pious people of the whole world as is evident from his travel experiences.

7.3 The End of the Punjabi National State

Had the rule of Maharaja Ranjit Singh's dynasty lasted for another couple of decades, Punjabees would have had a Punjab national state with capital at Lahore while rest of India would be struggling against the growing British stranglehold. There were internal reasons for the fall of the Punjab state. The king had the noble example of Secular governance by Akbar and the message of brotherhood of all Punjabees, but he could not get out of the morass of kingship that of keenness to keep the kingdom in the family or to handpick a successor. There was no precedent of identifying people as the successor and to crown the choice of the majority of the Punjabees. This had been the bane of all great kings and emperors including Harsh of Kanauj, Akbar of Delhi, Napoleon of Paris, or Aurangzeb, the last of the great Mughals. Even the Punjab kingdom based on the strength of the Khalsa could not unite all the Sikh rajas of Punjab. The cis -Sutlej states of Sikh rulers sought protection of the British rather than align with Maharaja Ranjit Singh. They were the bulwarks of the British colonial rulers in the initial advance of the great mutiny of 1857. They were fully rewarded by the tenacious colonial power. Many unhappy Sikh sardars found solace in their company in the colonial camp. In part, the ill luck struck Nau-Nihal Singh when he would have had the united loyalty of the Khalsa and other close relations in the royal family. The valiant fight of the Khalsa armies and the botched leadership of the mutually plotting ambitious Sardars for selfish ends ended in the annexation of the Punjab kingdom to the colonial regime of India. Credit must be given to the British administrators and army generals who not only pacified the Punjabees but won their loyalty to the British in spite of having lost political power to the British. They also very ably nipped all semblance of mutinous behaviour in the company troops all over the Punjab with over-awing cruelty. They strengthened the belief of Punjab armies in the ability of the British to overcome the mutiny which they did with the strong support of Sikh states of the Punjab and the inaction of Khalsa armies who in general were not unhappy with the crushing defeat of the rebellious Hindustani soldiers who had been the real base of enslavement of the Indian royal houses including that of the Punjab. The British speedily disarmed the Hindustani army of occupation in the Punjab and disarmed all Punjabees. They cancelled all jagirs requiring the Jagirdars to appear before British authority for fresh allocations. The British continued the Maharaja's administration and style of functioning by creating a Raja like aura about British collectors placed in each district. The begar or forced labour had particularly reached obnoxious limits during the rule of the Misls and the anarchy which had often overtaking the Punjab countryside. It was abolished. The Hindu bankers and money lenders and their trade flourished due to relatively strict rule of law so long as the British taxes and duties were not affected. The British boastfully engraved the challenge on a Lawrence statue at Lahore that "Do you want to be ruled by the pen or the sword".

The dream of a nation of Punjabees was extinguished also from the growing distance between the Muslim majority and the non-Muslim, Hindus and the Sikhs. The numerical strengths became very important when the British introduced a version of democracy based on religious labels and encouraged with every social and legal device conversions to Christianity. For spiritual advancement, only the active effort of the individual is involved. There could never be the necessity of learning a practically outlandish theology when vast theologies already existed in the country. Even the Christians of free India are re-learning and equating the ancient Jewish theology now with Indian theology and Indian gods and goddesses. (The Muslims had already done some spadework in this exercise and many Muslim *pirs* are equated to Hindu figures in rural Punjab or Bengal.) The Hindus took advantage of relative freedom after the excesses of the Afghan rule or recurring anarchy and gave vent to their old grievances by pushing the Muslims to partial untouchability gaining their natural reaction of anger and hatred. The British had held Muslims as prime movers of the mutiny and withdrew usual state concern for their advancement in professions or trade. The later day favours came only out of anger with Hindus and Sikhs for openly advocating end of the British rule. The Muslim landlords and titled toadies gave every sign of loyalty to the British. The British rule over whole of India and their concern like that of Aurangzeb in the integrity of India as an imperial possession gave India a nation status in the Imperial camp with all powers of war and peace staying with the India Office in London. The Punjab's dream of belonging to a free nation merged with the possibility of India emerging as a free nation. It is Bengal, Punjab and Gujrat that sharpened the tools of Swadeshi and boycott that in the hands of Mahatma Gandhi eventually encouraged the British to again count their profit and loss and quit India prodded by the revolutionary sentiment fostered by the Ghadar movement in the Punjab and Kisan morchas and petty mutinies all over India especially in the Royal Indian Navy. The communists who are now a respectable democratic force in all Asia as well as in India favour the unhindered progress of all "nationalities" of India which has also been the position of all major political parties of India when they have worked for and welcomed linguistic federating states in India. India has been able to retain the loyalty of the Jammu and Kashmir State on the promise of developing itself as a federation of fraternal states in mutual harmony and mutual support. Punjab will also flourish and perhaps reach the stature of ancient Harappan dimensions and happiness. In the dawning era of Indo-Pakistan cooperation, new ways of Punjabee togetherness will evolve out of SAARC in parallel with Bengalee "nationalism" which will also be a blessing for the India's North East region. But all this depends on the wisdom of the people of India including separatists in Kashmir, mulki sentiment of Andhra, Maharashtra and rebels in North East India and the communist conspirators in the tribal belt of central India and Bengal. To make India a nation and to satisfy the ambitions of all "nationalities"in the communist jargon, the patriotic Indians will have to make sacrifices. The Punjabees have a record of making sacrifices. They have to consolidate the national sentiment in the Punjab, Haryana, Jammu and Kashmir and other neighbouring states. For this the Punjabees have to do nothing new but only to keep on the narrow path of unselfish care of others as demonstrated by the great Gurus and the pious pirs and the caring folk of the Punjab. Hindus of the Punjab are one and all Sahajdhari Sikhs and should be permitted to demonstrate their faith in the Gurus. Senseless separatism of the Sikh "intelligentsia" is making Taliban of the Sikhs by authoritative statements discouraging young love and marriages of mixed couples. The mis-translation of the "Bhagoti ji" in the Sikh prayer has to be un-done. This can be easily achieved when genuine scholarship is utilized in the preparation of new word books of the Punjabi language. The rulers of cis-Sutlej Sikh states have made ample amends for siding with the central colonial rule of the British during the defeat of the mutiny, by vigorously helping the national integration of the Indian states in which the help of the ruler of Patiala and of Bikaner against the machinations of the British and Mr. Jinnah to balkanize India is to be acknowledged. They had to contend with British stooges like the Muslim rulers of Hyderabad, Bhopal and Junagarh states. The central government has to be strong and willing to curb any signs of anti-national activity like the recent anti-national activity of Bal Thackeray and his son creating riot conditions against north Indians in Maharashtra. They were negating the sacrifices of Sivaji and great Maratha freedom fighters under the Congress banner. The Punjabees should take the lead against all kinds of minority reservations but exert to bring up the competitive merit of all Indians. The Sikhs should be encouraged to think and function as leaders of Punjabees by service and merit. The Punjabees have to give the lead in creating a corruption free society. The Gurus spoke against tobacco. The Punjabees have to work against drinking and intoxicating drugs in addition especially among the impressionable youth.

7.4 Punjabees as Rebels against British Rule

After Punjab's annexation to the British empire, Punjabees generally thought it to be a tolerable fate compared to the lawlessness of the rule of local jagirdars. But many Sikhs would not be disloyal to the promise of Khalsa to bring about the rule of Waheguru through true Sikhs. The expression of their feelings came though unsuccessful plots to assassinate high British officials. Three great martyres Baba Bir Singh, Baba Khuda Singh and Baba Maharaj Singh, had to spend their lives as prisoners in the Andamans. An annual fair is held at Gurdwara Baba Bir Singh near Jammu. Nor can we forget the Nihangs who live still in their memories of the victorious Khalsa. They prefer living in the wilderness like the Lohars who were retrieved only recently from the darkness of their memories of Rana Pratap and Haldighati. The Nihangs take pride in the Sikh martial arts and horsemanship.

The most organized rebels were the Namdharis or the Kukas. Baba Ram Singh, the founder of the movement had started a parallel government. He preached boycott of all foreign institutions. Ninety-five Kukas were blown from the mouth of cannons at Malerkotla in 1872 where the Kukas had overthrown all colonial authority. A memorial postal cover could be issued in their honour to give a start to a festival occasion on their martyrdom day. There was disaffection also in important towns of the Doab. The Namdharis have a "Gaddi" near Ludhiana at Bhaini and have a Guru ruling the flock. The Namdhari Guru is highly respected since he boldly gave solace to the "do or die" volunteers of the quit India movement of 1942. Most Punjabees believed like Mahatma Gandhi that Indians should welcome the British victory in the First World War trusting them to do justly with loyal Indians and the Punjabees who were making so much sacrifice for such victory. The British, however, knew for certain that continuation of Indian empire under British control was the biggest return they could expect from the victory. Their rule in India and in the Punjab became more severe leading to black laws, Jallianwala Bagh tragedy and strong boycott and civil disobedience movements in the Punjab. The Punjab revolutionaries also became active. Ghadar party was organized and Lala Hardayal, the first editor of the news sheet Ghadar was arrested and externed to USA. The Kamagata Maru incident followed. The Sikhs had found welcome opportunity of migrating to California or to the west coast of Canada but were finding obstacles on the way. The ship Kamagata Maru was privately hired to take Indian migrants to Canada, but was repeatedly denied passage by the British influenced foreign coastal authorities. Ultimately the ship was forced to return to Calcutta where the British Indian police arrested and scattered all the people on board. This gave rise to tremendous awakening in the country to their lot as a slave country of the British. Many Ghadarites were now either in prison or in the front ranks of Gandhian Civil disobedience. The leftists became educators for rebellion in India with the help of newly formed Communist world-wide movement. The frustrated Indian princes were already trying to reach out to the Bolsheviks for helping them regain control of their states. Leftist leaders from Punjab, Muslim revolutionaries of present Pakistan, and Afghan revolutionaries were gathering at Kabul and petitioning through representatives stationed at Tashkent for the Bolsheviks to attack on the British in India with their active support. The whole thing fizzled out because of the communists preoccupation with consolidation within the Soviet Union.

There was an imposition of an all British Simon Commission to pronounce new control measures. Lala Lajpat Rai's death from brutal Police charge on the procession at Lahore led by him against this was the last straw on the heap of atrocities borne by the people. It led to open rebellion by Bhagat Singh and his band of revolutionaries. Their violence also had a word of praise from Mahatma Gandhi for their bravery and love of their country and the poor of the world. Rest is recent history. How the country marched to freedom coupled with last ditch conspiracy of the British to partition it and to create the infamous communal divide which is still haunting India and Pakistan which was created to weaken the voice of reason and a voice raised against injustice anywhere in the world. But human destiny of development and progress has prevailed and both India and Pakistan are in the process of finding wisdom in each other's welfare and are hoping to assist progress and development in the entire world spreading true peace and goodwill everywhere.

7.5 Chronology of Punjab History

521 B.C.	Darius reaches Multan and Lahore.
126 B.C.	Hindu-Buddhist kingdom ruled by Greek king Milinda of Buddhist literature.
323 B.C.	Invasion of Alexander blunted by Porus at Jhelum, and Punjab tribes at Beas and near Multan.
50 B.C	Hindu rule at Taxila 19-45 A.D. Indo-Parthian Hindu-Buddhist rule in western Punjab.
65 A.D.	Kushans supplant Parthians.
175 A.D.	End of Kushan rule (of Kanishka and his son Havishka).
372 A.D.	Tomar Rajpoots re-build Delhi old fort.
490	Death of Dharmagiri of a Jammu dynasty, that ruled Punjab for 400 years.
550	Battle near Multan when Raja Salwahan of Punjab expelled the Scythians (Buddhist by profession)
650	Kashmir ruler also ruled at Taxila.
840- 912 A.D.	Raja Bhoj of Kannauj gave power to his ministers known as Mehtas, Raja Bhoj was contemporary of Jaipal Shahi of Kabul.
850	Hindu Shahis rule at Kabul.
887	Anand Pal of Kanauj went to assist Shahis of Kabul but had to fall back to Peshawer where he lost a decisive battle.
1026	Extinction of Hindu Shahi kingdom at Kabul.

1186	Ghauri expelled the governor set up by Ghaznavi at Lahore. Awars' and Khokhars' sway in mountainous west Punjab.
1239	Razia Begum Sultan of Delhi killed at Bathinda in civil war.
1241	Mughals occupy Lahore at the invitation of a Razia Partisan in the Civil war
1398	Taimur conquered Ravi-Chenab region of Punjab. Shaikh Khokhar ruled at Bhimber and got appointed as governor by the Delhi Sultanate.
1426-1456	Pathans and Mughals battle for Delhi throne till Akbar wins.
	Punjab under governors appointed by Mughals and then by the King of Afghanistan who came to help against Marathas and Sikhs. Sikhs succeeded in throwing out both Pathans and Mughals as rulers.
1579	Abolition of Jaziya tax on Hindus by Akbar.
1679	Resumption of the tax.
1707	Death of Aurangzeb.
1708	Assassination of Guru Govind Singh.
1707-1712	Dispersal of the Mughal empire.
1739	Nadir Shah sacks Delhi.
1761	Marathas decimated at Panipat.
1799-1839	Ranjit Singh's empire with Lahore as capital.
1824-1883	Swami Dayanand, Arya Samaj formed in 1875.
1845-1849	Anglo-Sikh wars.
1865-1876	Widespread famine.
1885	Indian National Congress formed.
1909	Separate Electorates introduced by the British.
1919	Jallianwala Massacre.

1921	Dyarchy introduced.
1928	Arrival of Simon Commission.
1939-1946	First World War.
1940	Muslim League passes Pakistan resolution.
1941	League calls for direct action.
1947	Freedom and partition of India. *
1949	Merging of states.
1949-56	Various Akali Morchas resulting in Punjabi Suba.
1953	Chandigarh built and occupied.
1956	Reorganization of states.
1966	Present Punjab carved.
1972	Simla Agreement.
1985	Orgaization of SAARC. Mr. Jinnah before his death expressed his dis-allusionment with Pakistan. Up to 1930, the Muslim League meetings failed due to lack of quorum. In 1930, Muslims of U.P. were jointly worshipping *Devi* for protection against epidemics. Altaf Husain, the leader of Muslim Muhijirs (migrants) from India to the Sind province of Pakistan condemned the partition of India engineered by the British with the help of gilded Muslim toadies.

7.6 The Separatist Movement led by Bhindranwala

The successful carving of a Muslim Pakistan from India fired the imagination of some Sikhs especially NRI Sikhs in Canada to achieve a small region in western districts of Punjab (I) where Sikhs outnumbered the Hindus as independent Khalistan. They also had the example of violent success of the Jews in Palestine. Within India the separatists also hoped to achieve the leadership of the Sikhs which had become a routine for the Akalis who had led the Gurdwara movement in the Punjab. Bhindranwala, an important leader of the Sikhs belonging to one of the strong *takhts* of the Sikhs in the Punjab played on the need of the Congress being harassd by Akali threats of protest movement for a significant Punjabi Suba within India, got a reprieve for his excesses against Hindus and Sikhs in pursuit of his communal policies and became still more noted leader of the Sikhs. His violent movement occupied Darbar Saheb as a centre of conspiracy and collection of arms to be used for a violent rebellion to wrest control of his proposed Khalistan. At one stage the Sikh terrorists were imposing road curfew for travel of the Hindus and many Hindus were pulled out of buses and shot in order to terrorize the public to surrender Khalistan to Bhindranwala. The terrorists were ruling many areas in the Punjab and Chandigarh after dusk and ranged up to the Terai area in the north of U.P. where Sikhs were now owning many farms. They had the town of Batala near Amritsar practically cut off from the security ring around Batala and Amritsar. Ultimately the virtual rebellion of Bhindranwala terrorists was suppressed by military action and in revenge the terrorists managed to kill Mrs. Gandhi, the Prime Minister of India. They had also murdered the Hindu head of the Department of Punjabi Studies of Panjab University primarily because their conspiracy was to mis-translate a Punjabi word Bhagoti that showed that the Sikh faith was rooted in Hindu beliefs. It would be natural for any revising Sikh intellectuals to make correction in the Punjabi dictionary.

The fascist movement of Bhindranwala set back national integration and Punjabees now live in semi-autonomous states of the North West and have to re-discover cooperative development of the North West India along with the north west of Pakistan.

8 PUNJABEES AND PUNJAB

8.1 Punjabee Brotherhood

The Punjabee brotherhood is the scattered descendants of the ancient people who occupied parts of India and Pakistan when the Vedic Hinduism overlapped and co-existed with the Harappan civilization. Important additional streams that flowed into these lands making one people along with the natives, were the Hun invaders from the north and some Turkish and Iranian tribes entered Afghanistan and Punjab after first being converted to Hindu-Buddhism. There was later an intrusion by force, of certain Bloch and Afghan tribes first convertd to Islam and to the belief that the Punjabees were anti-religious since they were idolaterous and were undeserving of the wealth and ability they possessed. The presumed moral superiority helped them to spread a Muslim empire over the Punjabi territories in spite of the heroic resistance of the Punjabees. Along with the Muslim invaders came the colonizers who struck roots in the new lands and also came the darveshes, and Sufi saints who engaged in competitive pious living with native Punjabees and thus gained more converts to Islam or rather more so personal following as pirs or gurus in the local dialect meaning living guides and dependable masters. Even when Hinduism was dressing itself in stiff rules of conduct and pushing many groups into high caste seclusion or casteless untouchability, a common Indian folk culture spread in the villages without any turmoil and friction. This was the situation when Punjabees generally prospered in the early decades of the twentieth century compared to the rest of the Indians and on a map of India the Punjab and Punjabi states constituted most of the Punjabee occupied area.

The present Punjab, the named area of Punjabees is a truncated Indian state. For Punjabees to contribute to the well-being of the world in general and India in particular with the historical Punjabi vigour and tenacity, they have to overcome the divisions imposed on them by history. First priority is to spread the Punjabi language in all Punjabee areas of old by non-official means. Punjabees are ahead in creating wealth and jobs through private enterprise in all these areas. Good Punjabi literature should be distributed with glossaries for Hindi knowing public. The Punjabi University at Patiala with goverment funds could be the apex organization for this purpose. Punjabi study circles using one or more of the common scripts to write or read Punjabi language, i.e. Gurmukhi, Urdu, Hindi or English could be set up. Punjab government could pioneer in holding sports meets and cricket matches of teams from the Punjabee area holding free documentary shows about full blown Punjabi culture and the Sikh Gurus and their exploits. The position of the Sikh Gurus and the Khalsa aims will always remain the crown of Punjabee ideals of pure worldly life. The asceticism of the Jains, logical analysis of the Buddhists and the easy adaptability with all human thought of the Hindus are all to the greater glory and public service of the Punjabees.

8.2 Folk Culture

Punjabees can best serve secularism by unstinted support of folk culture. The teachings of the Gurus, Kabir and Sufi Pirs and their poetry and songs constitute the basis of folk culture. Folk culture includes worship of Pirs, tombs and relics (a relic itself of worship of the Buddhist stupas spread all over Asia of ancient times). When reasonable precautions are taken not to disturb the meditation of others or the Namaz of the

Muslims, devotional or even all music is food for the soul and it is the essence of folk religion. Guru Nanak spread his word by songs and sublime poetry. Sublime poetry is also the vehicle used by the Koran. A secularist should consider himself lucky when allowed to participate in folk song fests.

Punjabi folk songs are rich in sentiments of love, family relations and jealousies or attachments, pulls of the mother and the wife, jokes and satires. There are songs of leisure and easy banter of girls or boys, favourite songs of valour and chivalry are always a good draw. Punjabi patriotic songs contributed to the attraction of political meetings and protest meetings during the nationalist struggle. Folk dances especially Bhangra, Gidda or Jhumar are the main attraction in rural entertainment along with rural sports and jugglery and stage conversation of professional entertainers. Punjabi calendar is studded with local or national holidays and festivals. Popular ones being Baisakhi, Dewali, and numerous bathing festivals.

8.3 Scientific Attitude and Scientific Approach

Whatever else they may do, Punjabees would serve themselves and others best by remaining anchored with scientific attitude and approach. A scientist never will agree to finality of any knowledge conveyed to him by human means. He is always prepared to jettison any information that no longer satisfies his reason or conscience. The Gurus recommend success in worldly life. The world is more and more involved with science and technology. Mathematics and science are the key to future progress. And the Punjabees must develop these talents in their children.

The ancient start in science and technology was smothered by excessive possessiveness of knowledge and deliberate policy of distrust of the masses who were discouraged in every way from becoming knowledgeable and dislodging the Brahmans in their monopoly of learning.

Indian scholarship also suffered from excessive submissiveness to elders and teachers and from wrong turn given to astronomy by linking it to astrology. Once the future generations start learning science in earnest, many advantages will flow. The greatest superstition that needs thorough exposure is the ancient belief in re-birth which is a sinker on the populace for crossing the sea of life if goal is freedom and betterment by own efforts supplemented by the education and many beneficial welfare schemes floated by the state and the national government.

8.4 Punjabees as Friendly Hosts

The lands of the Punjabees are destination for tourism both of Indians and foreigners. There is the famous Sikh religious circuit, archaeological sites related to Harappan culture, Ramayana and Mahabharata sites. Many are not aware that Sita was born near Patiala. Luv, the son of Rama founded Lahore and Kush the younger son founded Kasur, Vyas and Balmiki Ashrams still exist in the Punjab, circuit of Kurukshetra contains more than 300 sites related to Mahabharata and Hindu mythology. Same holds for Punjab (P). Indian and other pilgrims would love to visit ancient Hindu-Buddhist sites in NWFP or in Punjab (P) and Sind like the Moksha pool at Katasraj near Malot or the ancient temples still existing in Multan or the archaeological sites in Bannu and Peshawer districts, e.g. the Shah ji ki Dheri or the Bahawalpur Stupa. All such sites including Taxila and sites related to folk heroes: Raja Harish Chandra, Guga pir, Guru Gorakhnath and Heer-Ranjha dot the Punjab region of India and Pakistan.

There are Sufi edifices all over East as well as West Punjab. Many national laboratories have been built in the Punjab and in Haryana. Himachal Pradesh is another Rajasthan in regard to temples, arts, and nature's bounty. There is the lilting rhythm in Himachali folk music and folk dances. There are innumerable village deities and fairs.

Punjabees particularly the Muslims of west Punjab make excellent friends and hosts. In fact all Punjabees are of open and outgoing nature. They are adaptable as is seen from the welcome they get as settlers in foreign countries. They pick up foreign languages easily. Punjabees particularly the Sikhs have an excellent sense of humour and most Punjabees like the Americans can join others in under-selling their own accomplishments giving a chance to themselves to learn from others. They are good sportsmen and love justice and fair play.

8.5 Secularism

The force cementing together all Punjabees is that of secularism. Secularism means a welcome co-existence of all religions and philosophies. It means respect for all religions. Secularism is wrongly understood by some as being irreligious or being atheist. A secular person could be atheist without any inferiority complex. In fact more people in the world are counted as atheists than theists. The Buddhists and Jains find no role in the universe for God. Secularism is not a dogma to be sworn to. It is an approach accepting that world continuously changes and knowledge is expanding. No religion can include all knowledge or believe that some of the things contained in it cannot stand revision and improvement. Like in science and technology, when experience so dictates, earlier concepts must give way to superior ones. One can be secular or not, but no one can be pseudo secular. A secularist does not deny himself the advantages that may accrue through prayer. A prayer apparently addressed to the deity is in fact a conversation with one's ownself. Secularism is opposed only to the fundamentalism of all communities. Fundamentalism is the cloak of all fanaticism. A godless communist often a fanatic about the inevitability of victory over capitalism accepts as reform the dismantling of state interference with the market forces. The secularist is pragmatic and society's advance is the priority.

There was every chance that India and Pakistan could be set on separate independence without internal or external discord on the issue. The leaders who were negotiating had agreed to the partitioning of the country, but the apple cart was overturned by the fanatics when rioting was begun in NWFP which snow balled into ethnic cleansing of Pakistan and subsequently as retaliation in Punjab and Bihar. Mr. Jinnah, a secularist at heart died completely disillusioned with what he had achieved. After considerable cost to both countries, India and Pakistan are now discovering advantages in secularist co-existence and mutual assistance. The ambitions of Khalistani fanatic elements also are now in retreat. The Historical bonds between Sikhs and non-Sikhs are too strong to be blown away. The folk religion is a better guide for togetherness than the scriptural practices of high religion. Nanak, Farid and Kabir and their like are the teachers worth following in the interest of peace and prosperity. Let us look at everyone as noble, i.e. as a gentleman or as a lady.

8.6 Development of North West India

Rapid development is possible by cooperation of all Punjabees across state and internationl lines which should be quite possible in the growing environment of cooperation and multi-national enterprise. There are growing inter-regional councils and regional cooperation entities like the SAARC. Laws should be democratically laid down by acceptance of all concerned. India has to nip at start any slogans or tendencies that judicate reversion to self before public good. North West India is luckier than North East India since there is no inter-district or inter-state anarchy. The States have only to pursue their development plans framed preferably districtwise seeking cooperation from state and national bodies. India and Pakistan have now considerable scientific and technical know-how. There is no dearth of multi-national funds; each state can go its way regarding political parties and coalitions by them, but keep education and training in science and technology and development planning unhampered by bureaucratic and political interference. Education is a sacred task for human advance and has to be free of communal and linguistic bias.

Now that hurdles are off from supply of central Asian or Iranian gas across Pakistan and Afghanistan, the gas will first reach the north west region in India and if they do their planning in advance, they will speedily advance in industrialization. Such a spurt in industrial advance is now only few years away and land reservation for this spurt can proceed now in planned intensive use for establishing new institutions and factories to run for twenty-four hours, use of maximum automation and highly trained staff to be provided living environment of international standard. We have luckily satisfactory experience of integrating agricultural extension, rural development, gender equality, cooperative movement of women, health and sport enthusiasm. All these can be multiplied if there is a will. Future is assured for technically advanced and socially outgoing people like the Punjabees living in North West India.

GLOSSARY OF LESS FAMILIAR WORDS

Arya Samaj

An organization set up in the Punjab by the admirers and followers of Swami Dayananda in 1885. It has ten principles by which the members agree to mould their conduct. Swami Dayananda's teachings are contained in *Saṭayarth Prakash*. He believed the divine gift of the Vedas contains elements of all true religions and *Bhagwad Gita* to contain the summary of true faith. Arya Samaj accepted the Quranic teaching that worship of idols as prevalent in Sanatan Dharma was incorrect and God can be addressed in silent prayer or by recitation of chosen Ved Mantras in the morning and evening. The Arya Samaj is a social and religious organization. It followed the Christian practice of holding Sunday morning prayer and religious discourse sessions. It does not believe in human intermediaries between God and an individual and is against handing one's conscience to a Guru or preceptor. It also argues its beliefs from the touchstone of reason supported by Vedic truths.

In present India it has demonstrated the importance of science and technology for human advancement and pioneered in the setting up of many educational and technical institutions under the banner of Dayananda Anglo Vedic institutions or Gurukuls on the imaginary pattern of ancient Vedic period educational madrassas set up as living in schools from child's age of 5 years to adolescence. Arya Samaj enjoins strict celibacy of men below the age of 25 and of women below the age of 16 following the Brahmachari Ashram of human life. It has been a reformist organization and a fore-runner of agitation against inequality of women and scheduled caste Hindus. It also authorized conversion back into Hindu mould all who would like to return to man's natural calling that of Vedic Hindus.

Baloch

Baloch or Baluch is an inhabitant of Balochistan, a province of Pakistan with Sind in the east and Iran in the west. There are Baloches living across the border with Iran also. The Baloch dialect is possibly related to Dravidian languages and Baloch writing is akin to old Sumerian writing. Balochistan is a poor underdeveloped region, whose mineral wealth is not adequately assessed. Quetta is the capital city and Urdu the court language.

Daitya

A Daitya in Indian myths is one who has evil intentions regarding the human race. He is enemy of the gods who wish the human beings well-being especially when the human beings obey and worship the gods.

Dalit

A Dalit is one who is poor or belongs to a down-trodden social group, e.g. a scheduled caste, or a scheduled tribe eking out their livelihood with difficulty.

Ghadar

Literally mutiny or rebellion. Name of a party in early 20th century India that promoted rebellion from British rule. Also it is the name of a periodical published by Indian patriots in exile in USA and connected with Kamagata Maru efforts to emigrate desirous Punjabi fortune hunters to Canada against the wishes of the British government of India.

Hakim, Vaids

Hakim is a physician in India following the indigenous system based on ancient Greek traditions amplified by Asian professionals. Hakim also means an intellectual of good social standing. Vaids are medicine men following the ancient Hindu system of medicine known as Ayurveda.

Hindu-Buddhism

Buddha was born a Hindu and imbibed Hinduism of his day. He questioned the blind adherence to the Vedas as divine scriptures for the human beings. He even had doubts of a presiding deity over whole creation. The creatures follow their own nature and are reborn according to the crop of deeds that they sow. Emancipation from pain, the lot of creatures, is through suppression of desires and through treading the narrow path of virtue and discipline. He established the Sangha or the guiding association of his followers. His followers called themselves Buddhists but were not converts. Hindus readily recognized the virtue of Buddhist logic and incorporated the Buddha in their list of godly persons granted to elevate the lot of the Hindus. The Historians wrongly separate the Hindu period of Indian history from the intervening Buddhist period. In Bengal the ruins of ancient structures cannot identify the original structure to be Hindu or Buddhist. These were clearly Hindu-Buddhist. The export of Buddhism to countries outside India was also an export of Hindu-Buddhism. In Japan Buddhist temples did not usually include distinguishing Hindu symbols, but the Japanese Shintoism was a clear echo of Indian Hinduism and the temples had the Shinto-Buddhist flavour. Many Indian dynasties had rulers who were personally inclined to Buddhism but the overall dynasty stayed Hindu-Buddhist. It is historically incorrect to see internecine warfare in India in the intervention of suspected Buddhist period in the overall Hindu period of history. The relation of Hindus with Buddhists was of the same kind that exists even now between the Hindus and the Jains. Jains agree with Buddhists regarding the Vedas or the position of God as a concept of a particular well argued philosophy but God has no objective existence. Common Hindus revere the Buddhist monks and the Sangha as well as the Jain Munis and their ideals of non-violence and asceticism. Indian culture is equally evident in ancient cave quarters of Hindu, Buddhist or Jain monks.

Hukamnamas

Literally orders that must be obeyed by the faithful flock. The Sikhs have endowed democratic authority to Akal Takht (an institution of the Sikhs established at Amritsar independent of their Golden Temple) to issue Hukamnamas when the Sikh masses needed to pursue a particular policy.

Jagir, Jagirdar

Jagir is the authority to collect revenue from certain land or village on behalf of the ruler. Jagirdar is the agent who has been granted the Jagir. A common practice of the Indian kings was to allot Jagirs for meritorious service in the army or otherwise. The British in India upheld the system. The present government does not recognize old Jagir rights beyond what are granted to all Indians. The British also introduced the grant of civic titles which is now continued through Padam Shri etc. awards not to be used as title.

Jogis, Sanyasis

Jogis are ascetics who also practice meditation in the Hindu, Buddhist, Jain or Muslim style. Jogis do not answer to any calling of caste or religion having renounced worldly life.

The Sikhs look down on renunciation of the world but all Indians respect the Jogis or Sanyasis who at ripe old age take to Sanyas after renouncing the world.

According to the Vedic ordering of human life, the last quarter of life should be spent as a Sanyasi away from worldly pursuits, immersed in meditation and joy of creation. The modern thinkers of India are against renunciation of the world and want the entire life to be spent on learning and constructive work for the uplift of the public and the country.

Khalsa

Guru Gobind Singh, the tenth Guru of the Sikhs, turned them into Khalsa through an initiation ceremony when each individual was made a sacrifice for Sikh ideals in the hands of the guru. Khalsa term also applied to the Sikh armies that outfought the Mughals and Pathans in the Punjab. In the Anglo-Sikh wars the Khalsa won the admiration even of the enemy. The history of India might have been different, if the great Indian mutiny had occurred when the Sikh force was intact, i.e. a few years earlier.

Kuru Niti

Kuru Niti refers to the Punjabi ethical doctrine that was common currency in the Punjab of the Kurus before and after the Mahabharata war fought at Kurukshetra. Kuru Niti really is the ethics of the heroes of epic quality visible throughout the text of the Mahabharata. It is believed that the Buddha imbibed it when sojourning with Jain ascetics or when visiting north-west India as a pilgrim before his enlightenment.

Mahayana, New Mahayana

Mahayana form of Buddhism originated in Kashmir and was

the drive for the appearance of a vast Buddhist empire in West Asia with capital cities of Peshawer and Taxila in India. The new philosophy realizing the importance of prayer in everyone's life, allowed Buddhists to worship the Buddha and to meditate on various Bodhisattvas or local gods. A universal religion allowed universalism in worship creating a unity in diversity. This later led to inclusion of planets and magic and later to Hindu, Muslim and Buddhist Tantra and thus diluted the elevating push of religion. In India much of folk religion is still based on miracle mongering, but folk religion has an appeal for all secularists accepting the limited nature of appeal of high religion and the holding and refurbishing quality of folk religion. The New Mahayana is an extension of Mahayana to include co-existence not only of many gods but also of various political and economic theories.

Mustopia

From advances in geophysics it is becoming clear that there is no likelihood of an end to the universe in only a few centuries. The earth and the sun are going to last for few billion years more and the possible natural dangers like earthquakes, tsunamis, abnormal weather, glaciation etc. will be temporary setbacks in limited areas and a united and cooperating world can fend such calamities or ride over them. With the evidence of progress made in the last two centuries, international peace and self-interest of the human race assure continued scientific and technical advance assuring a glorious future of peace and plenty. Such inevitable utopia has been termed mustopia by the author. All nations can now on, adjust their policies and plans to be responsible citizens in the mustopia. Inernational U.N. governance through independent and enthusiastic nations have to be established along with restructuring of the social scene through continuous rise in living standards and well distributed entertainment for all. India is already embarked on this road when they assure necessities to all its billion population. Soon mustopia political parties will supplant the green parties of yester year all over the world. In mustopia, religion will square up with the findings of science and technology.

Muths or Maths

Muths or Maths are religious establishments on the lines of Vihars established by the Buddhist Sangh. Hindus, Jains and Christians have many such institutions. A vibrant example is the Radha Soami Satsang at Beas near Jalandhar. Many religious mission stations are practically muths.

Netaji

Literally respected leader or fuhrer (in German). This was the way, the adoring public chose to address Netaji Subhas Chandra Bose when he decided to use force for expelling the British rule from India. He raised a fighting National force in East Asia for attacking British in India from the east in alliance with the axis powers, chiefly the Japanese who had handed over volunteers for him from among the Japanese held Indians as prisoners of war when the Japanese over-ran East Asia in the beginning of the World War.

Puranas

The Puranas are Hindu holy books in which the ethics is taught through stories and myths connected with Hindu pantheon of many gods and their families. Puranas are written by learned authors in all periods of Hindu existence. There is a *Bhavishya Purana* dealing with future deeds of God-incarnate who will appear on the scene to give a final spread of godliness to whole mankind. Some Muslims believe that the Qadiani leader of Punjab was the Kalki Avatara fore-told in the *Bhavishya Purana*. The Muslim divines of Pakistan have declared Qadianis to be non-Muslims.

Pushtun, Pashto

Pushtun or Pakhtun are Pashto or Pakhto speaking tribe residing across the border with Afghanistan. The Frontier Gandhi, Khan Abdul Gaffar Khan, the leader of nonviolent Khudai Khidmetgars (literally servants of God) and himself an ardent admirer and friend of Mahatma Gandhi was a Pushtun leader. He mourned the creation of Pakistan and his followers still labour for a secular regime in Pakistan and must have welcomed the down turn for the fanatic Taliban in Afghanistan.

SAARC

South Asian Association of Regional Countries. It is one of similar regional associations set up to be a link between nations and United Nations for development programmes and for regional cooperation within the UN umbrella. SAARC is likely to gain momentum now that India and Pakistan are not at loggerheads.

Sahajdharis

Sahajdhari (Sikhs) are Hindu Punjabees who venerate the Sikh Gurus and donated their eldest boys to the Sikh faith when they were subjected to oppression by the Mughal governors of Sirhind and Lahore. They continued in this and in donating their wealth to the Sikh funds but did not wear the symbols of Sikh faith prescribed by the tenth Guru.

Sanatan Dharma

Sanatan Dharma literally means the ancient human duty. It

stands simply for humanism. Hindus are of Sanatan Dharma first and later of any other calling or adherence to any formal religious beliefs or principles. As humanist, a simple next step is to be secular and adhere to a convincing proposition not interfering with their humanism and secularism. Sanatan Dharmis are convinced about the existence of God, soul, and transmigration of souls, existence of heaven and hell for temporary shelter of souls while waiting for rebirth. They also have faith in miracles and assign all kinds of miracles to their respected great religious men or women. They have use of personal gurus and preceptors besides holy books. The personal guru can belong to any religious calling. They love to join in any worship as the *Gita* teaches them that all worship reaches the same one God. They have space for many gods and love to worship idols in temples or featureless God in silent or vociferous prayers and singing or meditation. A Hindu has no place for conversion but will take to any religious course that satisfies him or his already adopted guru. Sanatan Dharma is a religion of freedom and free thinking. Life and creation fascinate him and he is keen to reconcile his thought and experiences with advances in science and technology.

Sarvodaya

Sarvodaya literally stands for the dawn of cultural and material advance of all. The word was often used by Mahatma Gandhi when stating his concept of human advance. He emphasized that the advance has to be felt by the lowliest of the low in existing dispensation.

Sharia

Muslims aim is to mould a human being into a clone of their prophet who had direct contact with God. All his actions and sayings are dutifully collected and referred to for actions and sayings of the prophet Mohammed. An advice rising from Sharia is like a Hukamnama or a sacred order.

Sunni, Shia

Sunni and Shia are the two main sects among Muslims differing only in the enumeration of Imams or religious and temporal dignitaries of Islam who succeeded to the leadership after the passing away of Hazrat Mohammed. The Shias were treated as rebels by Sunni power and decimated at Karbala battle. Shias are a majority only in Iran, but have influential minority in certain countries especially India and have a majority in the Indian state of Jammu and Kashmir Shias remember their martyrs of Karbala battle by mourning processions carrying paper-board memorials.

Stupa

A stupa is a memorial pillar planted at many sites by Buddhists, particularly the emperor Ashok instructing the public in the ethical way of life propagated by him, an ardent Buddhist. Stupas are unearthed all over Buddhist lands from old times, e.g. India, Pakistan and Afghanistan or west Asia and certain parts of China, Stupas are constructed these days only in Nepal or Myanmar.

Tabligh

The Tabligh was a conversion movement started in the Punjab by Muslims in response to the Shuddhi movement for reconversion into Hinduism (Arya Samaj) after the communal electorates had been introduced in the country. In the new climate of adult suffrage and secularism of India conferring no special rights and consideration for any religion, Tabligh and Shuddhi movements have no relevance. In India conferring no special rights and consideration for any religion, Tabligh and Shuddhi movements have no relevance. In India religious conversion has to be purely to self-selected religion for more spiritual peace.

Ulema

Ulema are the respected Muslims who have thorough knowledge of Islamic Sharia. Ulema function in Islam as the ultimate judicial adviser.

BIBLIOGRAPHY AND NOTES

India 2006

Major irrigation is by tube wells in Punjab, more than 1000 solar pumps are operating. Bicycle parts cluster organization at Ludhiana. Festivals : Maghi Mela at Muktesar. Basant festival at Patiala, Hola Mohalla at Anandpur Sahib. Urs of Roza Sharif at Sirhind, Harvallabh Sangeet Sammelan at Jalandhar.

Pakistan Almanac, Royal Book Co., Karachi.

Damodar wrote Heer Ranjha in verse during the time of Akbar. Sultan Bahu (d.1691) wrote mystical poetry. Bulley Shah of Heer Ranjha fame died in 1758, Folk romances are ever popular, e.g. Heer Ranjha, Sasi Punnu, Sohni Mahiwal, Mirza Saheban. Also Dohas and kafias and poetry of Habib Jalil.

Archaeological Survey Publications (Agroha, Gandhara, Survival of pre-historic Civlization of Indus valley : Memoir No. 41, Kuru Kshetra, Mathura, Panchala.) Vratyas were Kshatriya by caste, and Yatis were wandering mendicants. Bhrigus and Atharvans taught fire cult. The Buddha taught that austerities were not necessary for piety. There was a cult (still surviving in Nepal) of standing pillars crowned by animal figures. Punjabi University, Patiala and its Historical Surroundings.

History of Porus Budh Prakashan, Punjabi University, Patiala.

Various District Gazetteers.

History of Punjab Hill States (Hutchinson and Vogel)

Aggarwal, J.C. and S.P. Aggarwal : *History of Punjab*, Concept Publishing Co., New Delhi, 1992

Ahmed Salim : *Punjab, Revisited,* Gautam Pub., Lahore, 1995

Ram Ahuja, *Society in India,* Rawat Pub., Jaipur, 2002

Bali, A.N., *Glimpses of Punjab History,* A.N. Bali Publisher, 1969

Balkrishna, M., *Kurukshetra,* P.R. Pub., 1978

Worship of serpents; Sthan Tiratha - popular with Janpad Shrikantha and the dynasty of Pushya Bhutis. There is belt of nine streams around Kurukshetra. Excavations at Karan ka Qila date from 2000 B.C. to 500 A.D. Akbar visited Kurukshetra in 1567 and observed sanyasis and jogis fight for alms. Nadir Shah plundered Kurukshetra in 1739. Marathas acquired control in 1754 and cancelled the jazia tax. Jaffar Mohammed of Thanesar was active in the Wahabi movement.

Bhati, H.S., *Folk Religion,* Rawat Publ., N.D., 2000

Present Punjabi society is dominated by Jats. Shrines of Kali, Naina Devi, Mansa Devi and Vaishno Devi are popular with all Punjabees.

S.R. Chatterji, *The Cultural Heritage of India,* Vol. 5. Institute of Culture, Kolkata

V.D. Chopra (Ed), *Pakistan and Asian Peace,* Patriot, Pub. New Delhi, 1985

J.B.Das-Gupta, *Islamic Fundamentalism,* Maulana Azad Inst. of Asian Studies, Kolkata. Radical Islam is opposed to liberation, is anti-Shia and anti-West. It is Wahabist. Sayyad Maududi founded Jamat-i-Islami in 1941. Shifted his abilities to Pakistan of Ayub Khan. Tunisia has demonstrated that fundamentalism could be defeated by secularist approach and industrial economy. They have outlawed polygamy, social pressure for fasts etc.

Devaputra (Ed.), *Historical and political perspectives.* Books and Books, N.D. 1982

Dimitriev, G.L., *Indian Revolutionaries in Central Asia,* Hope India Pub., 1982

Many unhappy with British rule in India found free atmosphere at Tashkent. Leaders of the Gadar party were

Har Dayal and Mohammed Barkatullah. Provisional government of India was set up at Berlin and at Kabul by Raja Mohinder Pratap. M.N. Roy travelled to confer with the Bolsheviks at Moscow.

Veena Dua, *Arya Samaj in Punjab Politics*, Picus Books, 1999. Was active in the uplift of Meghs (S.C.) and refugees from Pakistan. Set up DAV institutions, an example of self-help and modernization to others.

A. Fazl, *An Invitation to Ahmediyas, Quadian*, Pb. 1961

Budh Prakash, *Evolution of Heroic Tradition in Ancient Punjab*, P.U. 2001

Toyanbee theory that growth is maintained by creative minority. Societies that put brakes on new ideas harping on assumed perfection of existing knowledge doom themselves to stagnation and violence. Hazara used Landa script. Route through Baramula and Gilgit opened to Kashgar and through Zojila to Tibet and China. Jalalabad where river Kunal meets Kabul river is full of ancient Buddhist stupas. Gupta empire extended to the Oxus. Afghan mountains end at Bolan pass. Afghanistan was ceded to Mauryan emperor by Seleucus on his failed attack on the Indian empire. New fruits were introduced from Iran and China. In the centuries around the birth of Christ large scale reclamation of land took place in the plains of the Punjab. Hindu-Buddhist Kushanas brought in gold currency; trade flourished, but people were oppressed till they rebelled under the leadership of tribes of south-east Punjab. Growth of Indo-Afghan School of Art (Bamyan Buddhas destroyed by the Taliban to their eternal discredit.)

Gill, K.P.S., *Knights of Falsehood*, Har Anand Publ., N.D., 1997

Dr. S.P. Gupta, *The Punjab (An Overview)*, Ess Pee Pub., Chandigarh, 2004

J.B. Das Gupta, *Islamic Fundamentalism and India.* Inst. of Asian Studies, Kolkata, 2002

Indira Gandhi, *Eternal India*, B.T. Pub., Delhi, 1980

Hindus and Muslims in India worship at each others' shrines. Muslim priests at a Hanuman temple in Gujarat and at Amarnath Shrine in Kashmir.

Holland, E.A. (Ed.), *Modern Shrubs and Trees of Punjab*, Cambridge University Press, 1918

Jacob,T.G., *Chaos in Nation Formation*, Odyssey Pub., 1990

Joshi, L.M. and Fauja Singh, *History of Punjab I and II*, Punjabi University Patiala, 1977

Sixth century A.D. coins of Vasudeva found in Haryana and of Somdeva at Kabul. Copper hoard from Mithathal of Haryana.

Harbans Singh, *Heritage of the Sikhs*, Manohar Pub. 1983

Ranjit Singh vanquished the Afghans and secured the Koh-I-Noor from them. The ten gurus were : Nanak, Angad, Amardas, Ramdas, Arjun, Hargovind, Har Rai, Harkrishan, Tegh Bahadur, and Govind Singh who wrote in the Zafarnama that ethical principles should have supremacy in politics. Ranjit Singh crowned Maharaja at Lahore in 1799. Baba Dayal started the Nirankari way and held a Nirankari Darbar at Rawalpindi. Namdhari movement started by Bhai Balak Singh (1799-1860). Hazara district pogrom against the Sikhs in December 1946. Khan of Mamdot replaced Sikandar Hayat as Chief Minister at Lahore before 1947.

Kailash Mohan, *Militant Nationalism in the Punjab*, Manohar Pub. N.D. 1985

Rajiv A. Kapur, *Sikh Separatism*, Vikas Pub. New Delhi, 1987

Karan Raj, *Dictionary of Terrorism*, Sarup and Son, Delhi, 2002

Dev Kutti (Ed.), *Historical and Political Perspectives*, Books and Books, N.D.

Shiv Lal, *Date Line Punjab*, Election Archives, N.D., 1994

S.M. Latif, *History of the Punjab*, Kalyan Pub., N.D., 1989

Tomb of Sakhi Sarwar, a folk hero in Multan. Baba Farid of Pak Pattan. Khwaja Khizr, a folk deity. Mughals occupied Afghanistan with support of Gakkhars of Punjab. Taimur's invasion in 1398. Akbar got constructed special premises at Lahore for religious symposia and discussions. In 1644 the Mughal emperor conquered Balkh and Badkshan across snow covered mountains. Aurangzeb abolished the Navroz festival begun by Akbar. There was strict discipline in government in Shah Jehan's times, Highways were secure and there were no thefts. Aurangzeb disallowed singing, dancing and buffoonery entertainment. He banished the dance girls. A large Hindu temple near Delhi was set on fire. He destroyed temples in Varanasi and Mathura. A mosque was built near the site of the Mathura temple. He prohibited Shias from wearing long moustaches and expelled jogis and sadhus from Delhi.

Ahmad Shah Abdali in alliance with the Mughals chastised the rebellious governor at Lahore with assistance from the Raja of Jammu. He left Lahore in 1762 leaving one Kabuli Mal as governor. Sikhs looted Kasur and Malerkotla. Sikhs plundered Lahore in 1764. They levied Rakhi (protection) tax from all defeated chieftains in the then prevelant Maratha style. The Sikhs commanded Begar (free service) from everyone.

The British C-in-C of company forces was a guest at Prince Nau Nihal Singh's marriage. (Ahmed Shah was in service with Nadir Shah and served first as governor at Kandhar.)

L.S. Leigh, *Punjab and the War*, Govt. Press, Lahore, 1922

January 1915, plague epidemic in Jhang Division, Muzaffargarh had rebellion in Kaiser's name resulting in punitive police. Some "no recruiting" leagues, but had an aeroplane fund started for the war effort. Labana Sikhs were ardent recruits. Many recruits from Hissar and Mansehra. Aroras plumped for recruitment. 3000 men from criminal tribes volunteered to join the army. Great Hindu temples existed at Multan, Nurpur, Lahore, Kangra, Thanessar, Pehowa, Katasraj and Malot (near salt range). Mounds at Shah-ji-ki-Dheri near Peshawer

Siri Vihar, a ruined stupa in Bahawalpur state indicate ancient edifices. Sikhs had minted coins at many places in the Punjab.

R.C. Majumdar (Ed.), *Vedic Age*, Allen and Unwin.

Mohinder Singh (Ed.), *History and Culture of Punjab*, Punjabi Univ. Patiala Hun kings of Kashmir (e.g. Mehrgul) persecuted Buddhists.

Nanda, J.N., *Sufis and Bhaktas*, Sikhism & Comparative Religion, Vol. 20, pp. 49-51, 2001

Nijjar, Bakhshish Singh, *History of Babbar Akalis*, ABC Pub., Delhi, 1937

D.B. Pandey, *Shahis of Afghanistan and Punjab*, Hist. Res. Inst., Delhi, 2002

Payne, G.H. *A short history of the Sikhs*, Nirmal Pub., New Delhi, 1986.

Describes the rise of Ranjit Singh and after his death how anarchy spread in his kingdom leading to Anglo-Sikh wars and seizure of the Punjab by the British company troops in India. The war started through rumours based on mutual suspicion. The Khalsa took the plunge and crossed Sutlej in a declaration of hostilities. The Khalsa in spite of reckless bravery of the Sikh soldier was incapable of victory in the absence of good generals and proper military strategy and tactics. All pitched battles had ended in stalemate but immediate assistance reached the company forces and the better placed reserves did not reach the Sikhs. Through superior tactics and bold attacks, the company forces convincingly won victories at Aliwal and later at Subraon. Gulab Singh negotiated the surrender terms and paid the imposed war indemnity from his own funds and in lieu was assured of hereditary rule over Jammu and Kashmir. The British still desired continued existence of the Punjab state under their protection. The subordinate status was galling for some Sardars particularly holding almost full power at distant places like Multan and Peshawer. Mulraj started a revolt perhaps un-itentionally at Multan that led to the second Anglo-Sikh war and after defeats or half finished battles at Chilianwala and Rasul, the disputant Sher Singh surrendered at Rawalpindi. The Punjab was annexed by the British Governor General and the task of pacification of the Punjab and the Sikhs began in which the British rulers-cum-administrators were eminently successful. Mulraj was deported to Andamans but died on the way.

Peta, Piara Singh. *The Sikh Empire.* National Book Trust Delhi 1986

Banda Bahadur (1671-1741) came to Punjab in 1708 and fought Mughal authority till his capture and martyrdom in a brutal manner. Emperor Farrukh Sayyar had ordered killing of Sikhs on sight. Nadir Shah invaded India in 1739.

H.R. Phadke, *Haryana, Ancient and Modern,* Arora Pub., N.D., 1981

L.I. Rempal, *Ancient India and Pre-Muslim Central Asia,* Soviet Pub. Tashkent, Demons are an incarnation of chaos. Swan of Brahma and ram of Agni. Rudra had his double in Sogda. Zoroastrianism was pushed aside by ancient Mazdeism-cult of ancestors.

Bertrand Russell, *Impact of Science on Society,* Blackie and Son, 1952

S.C. Sharma, *Punjab, The Crucial Decade,* Nirmal Pub., N.D., 1957

Narain Sharma, Indo-Pak Future, *Gandhi Marg,* Vol. 27(No.1), 2005

Tariq Ali, *The Clash of Fundamentalists,* Rupa and Co., N.D., 2002

The question is raised as to why there has been no Islamic reformation. Islam has evolved a dictatorship of brain washed ulema who refuse to see the advances made by others and take pride in suppressing freedom of thought. (Pakistan is proud of its madrassas according to the P.M.)

Paul Titus (Ed.), Marginality and Modernity, Oxford University Press, 1996

Ahmed Saleem, *Punjab Revisited*, Gautam Pub., Lahore, 1995
Harbans Singh, *Heritage of the Sikhs*, Manohar Pub., N.D., 1983
Jagjit Singh, *The Sikh Revolution*, Bahri Pub., N.D., 1981
N.K. Singh, *Islamic History of Kashmir*, Gulshan Pub., Srinagar, 2000
Sanat Sing, *The Sikhs in History*, UN Books, N.D., 1993
B. Vivekananda, Building on Solidarity, Laven Books, N.D., 2000

Index